CONFERENCE
PLANNING

CONFERENCE PLANNING

Edited by

W. Warner Burke

Richard Beckhard

SECOND EDITION

University Associates
7596 Eads Avenue
La Jolla, California 92037
1976

CONTENTS

CONTRIBUTORS

RICHARD BECKHARD

Richard Beckhard Associates
New York
Sloan School of Management
Massachusetts Institute of Technology

KENNETH D. BENNE

Professor of Human Relations
Boston University

LELAND P. BRADFORD

Executive Director
NTL Institute

W. WARNER BURKE

Human Relations Consultant
Washington, D.C.

STEPHEN M. COREY

Professor of Education
Teachers College
Columbia University

SAMUEL A. CULBERT

Assistant Professor
Graduate School of Business
    Administration
University of California
Los Angeles

CHARLOTTE K. DEMOREST (Deceased)

Formerly of
Education Department
Federation of Protestant Welfare
    Agencies, Inc.

BETTY R. ELLIS

Assistant Professor
School of Education
University of Florida

GILBERT LEVIN

Assistant Professor
Department of Psychiatry
Albert Einstein College of Medicine
Yeshiva University

GORDON LIPPITT

Professor, Behavioral Sciences
The George Washington University

RONALD LIPPITT

Institute for Social Research
The University of Michigan

MARGARET MEAD

American Museum of Natural History
New York

CYRIL R. MILL

Program Director
NTL Institute

WARREN H. SCHMIDT

Assistant Dean
Graduate School of Business
    Administration
University of California
Los Angeles

EDITH WHITFIELD SEASHORE

Organization Consultant
Washington, D.C.

DAVID D. STEIN

Assistant Professor
Department of Psychiatry
Albert Einstein College of Medicine
Yeshiva University

PREFACE TO THE SECOND EDITION

If there has been the slightest doubt regarding the permanency of the conference as a medium of social intercourse, it can be erased; the conference is here to stay. Since the first edition of this book was published, the conference has continued to be a major vehicle for human interaction. However, there have been at least three changes: there are *more* conferences of all types than ever before; there is a greater *variety* of conferences; and there is even more active *participation* by conferees than in the late fifties and early sixties. At the annual conventions of the American Psychological Association, for example, which have been rather formal in format, there has been a trend toward such things as "roundtable discussions" and less emphasis on the reading of technical papers.

It is now not so much a matter of whether to have a conference, but what type of conference to plan. Thus, we have categorized the articles in this second edition according to different aspects of conferencing and included sections on technology and specialized conferences.

The papers which have been added to this second edition tend to be more specialized than the earlier articles. These newer papers, in most cases, have built on the knowledge from the earlier articles. The first edition has not been replaced, but rather supplemented.

Because the basic principles of planning and conducting an effective conference have changed very little, most of the articles from the first edition have been retained. For example, the article by Ronald Lippitt is over twenty years old, but the ideas and techniques presented are quite relevant; it is still important to analyze the effectiveness of group process in getting the work done. The paper by Bradford and Corey is based on training laboratories held at Bethel, Maine, before 1950, but many of the design ideas in that article are highly useful for today. Conducting a large meeting so that all participants can collaborate in decision making and problem solving is still difficult, especially in light of the fact that even greater demands for a "piece of the action" are now being made by participants.

The book is now divided into four sections. Section I deals with factors to be considered in planning the conference.

Probably the major factor is the participant himself. Cyril Mill gives us some insight here. His experience is both unsettling and challenging, since it looks as if the conferee of the seventies is going to be considerably more demanding. Benne and Demorest discuss, among other things, the conference participant's expectations before a conference and what the conference planner can do to meet these expectations. Beckhard provides helpful ideas for planning the details of the conference program itself. Gordon Lippitt's article on the multiple roles of the meeting planner clarifies some of the complexities of the various planning functions. Although Mrs. Mead's paper is written in the context of the small professional conference, her detailed treatment of pre-conference arrangements provides a checklist for many kinds of conferences. (It is interesting to note that some of her opinions on the conduct of a conference, e.g., expressing one's feelings, differ from most, if not all, of the other authors in this book.)

There is now a growing body of knowledge about the specific techniques one can employ to improve a conference. While there is only one new article added to Section II, future editions will probably include more. While Bradford and Corey's article and Lippitt's paper provide methods for improving large and small group meetings, Culbert and Schmidt present nine strategies, some "tried and true," others relatively new, for involving participants in large meetings. Beckhard briefly discusses several different techniques for evaluating the effectiveness of a meeting.

Section III describes five of the numerous variations in conference formats and purposes. Schmidt and Beckhard briefly discuss three of these and then cover in some detail the special fact-finding conference, which generates considerable data—ideas, opinions, information—for future planning and action. The problem-solving conference discussed by Burke and Ellis is useful for identifying, diagnosing, and providing alternative solutions to problems. This type of conference also emphasizes the plotting of action steps.

The convention as a special type of conference is still utilized extensively by many organizations, political and otherwise. Beckhard contrasts the traditional convention with one planned more effectively and involving participating members. The effective international conference is as crucial today, if not more so, as when Bradford wrote about one he attended in 1959. The article by Levin and Stein was included in this edition because it may represent a type of conference, or an effective use of the conference method, that will be needed and utilized more in the future. While this type of conference requires more risk-taking on everyone's part, it can help to alleviate some of the tension points and possibly solve some of the current problems facing our society. Their article addresses some of the concern raised in Mill's paper.

A conference typically involves many people, and since the planners can seldom personally see that all of the participants are involved all of the time, others must be trained to help. The two articles in Section IV discuss the training of group discussion leaders. Edith Seashore presents an overview of a design for training these leaders for a general conference, and Ellis and Burke explain a training design for group leaders for a special problem-solving conference.

W. Warner Burke
May 1970

PREFACE TO THE FIRST EDITION

In the past twenty years "conferencing" has become a major form of social intercourse in Western society. Trade and professional associations, business organizations, and public and voluntary institutions bring together, in meetings each year, tens of thousands of statesmen, scientists, salesmen, social workers, surgeons, stockbrokers, and superintendents to exchange ideas and information, collect and analyze statistics or "positions," plan industry or organization strategy, train and develop members in everything from "evolving a personal philosophy" to "skills in beekeeping."

Meetings have become the principal source of business for most resort hotels and for an increasing number of big-city hotels, and new industries have developed to service this giant activity. The multitude of meetings is necessitated by the fantastic increase in the complexity of doing business in a space-age world. Face-to-face communication, reflection, and sharing of news ideas must be programmed if the world's vast new knowledge is to be utilized. It is also necessary to slow down the pace and build in time for reflection and planning; this results in the scheduling of many more "retreat" type conferences.

These changing conference conditions have been accompanied by changing role requirements for those involved in a conference.

Planners today spend much more time than formerly in planning these activities: it is not at all unusual for a committee to work two years in the planning of a three-day meeting.

Moreover, new skills are demanded of planners in addition to knowledge of the subject matter. Planners must be sophisticated in the employment of methods of conducting meetings from the widely differing aspects of presentation and participation. Skills of discussion leadership and leadership training are often required as well as skills in staging. Techniques of fact finding and evaluation are also used in most conferences.

With the "discovery" of the importance of two-way communication between platform and audience, presenters have been compelled to adjust their roles and develop new skills— to use both prepared and spontaneous material effectively, to "field" questions to elicit audience participation in large meetings, to make productive use of new visual media.

However, it is the *audience participants* who have undergone the greater role change. From a tradition of passive listening, the expectation today is for active sharing—for participation in small face-to-face groups, question periods, seminars, case studies, committees, and the like.

Today's conference is more and more a collaborative venture among planners, program presenters, and audience members. To create such a conference requires the selection of an appropriate physical and psychological setting, the creation of appropriate methods for conducting the meeting, and the provision for on-the-spot fact-finding and steering mechanisms to ensure effective results, and, perhaps most important, the acquisition of collaborative skills so that necessary teamwork can be developed.

The readings in this volume have been selected to deal with these aspects of conference planning and conduct.

Richard Beckhard

SECTION I

PLANNING THE CONFERENCE

Conference Planning
for the Seventies

CYRIL R. MILL

There is now a cult of the present. Change has come about so rapidly and continues at such an accelerated pace that not only does the past seem distant, but many of the old solutions are irrelevant. Ask yourself, for instance, how you feel about the value of a savings account in a world of inflation. Or the merits of insurance or a fixed retirement plan. Can you justify disciplining children today as you were disciplined? How about premarital sex, family planning, the place of religious institutions in society? If your convictions are wavering, you are in tune with the times.

In the midst of temporariness, the future seems even more distant because it is so unpredictable. Solutions are felt to be for now, not forever. Experts are hard put to show that verities established even five years ago do not need to be re-examined in the light of new evidence. It is not surprising that the young resist and question most of the traditions and beliefs of the old. Having been swept back and forth in the current of contradictory opinion in regard to drugs, the pill, the war, marriage, to say nothing of modes of dress, and food additives, the motto on the back of a hippie hearse was inevitable: "Apple pie will make you sterile."

One of the prevailing attitudes among the young of today is a refusal to accept the existing pattern of life and thought merely because it exists. A corollary is that there is no virtue in obedience to authority. Such attitudes bode ill for those presently in authority or those, like conference planners, who may be in such a position temporarily. They are

3

in for a rude awakening if they assume that their opinions and recommended procedures will be automatically respected and obeyed. The concept of shared control must become an accepted dictum in the future. Respect and obedience are not old-fashioned, but they have become double-edged concepts, working best when the one who expects respect can give it. He who wants to exert control must share it.

In the fall of 1969, a four-day conference was planned for 100 graduate students from across a wide range of disciplines. The goal of the conference was to acquaint them with environmental problems, raise their level of concern, provide them with information from expert resources, and send them back to their campuses to spread the word to others. Although the conference results far exceeded these goals, the conference planners and trainers went through a series of agonizing confrontations in the process. Almost nothing worked as they had planned it.

The students repeatedly employed "guerilla theater" tactics to subvert the conference design. If a room were set up with chairs in circles, the students purposefully broke up the formation and formed their own groups upon entering. If a speaker were scheduled, someone called out from the floor that his topic was irrelevant to their work at that time. Instead of following the suggested procedure (discussing a speech, forming questions for the speaker in small groups) one participant summarily discarded this design, grabbed the microphone, and took over the meeting. When directions were given for the next activity, the running commentaries from around the room were laced with obscenities.

As we look at this kind of conference behavior, we can anticipate a need to rethink our models for conferences in the years immediately ahead. The purposes of conferences will change. There will be fewer information-giving sessions and more information exchange; fewer passive audiences and more participative groups. There will be a greater insistence by the participants that they be included in the planning. The conference conveners will be closely examined and constantly monitored for evidence of hypocrisy, gaps, between word and deed, policies incongruent with practice, and tendencies to impose, indoctrinate, or coerce. The expectation will be for plans of action; few will be satisfied with the feeling that, "We got together and heard some inspirational speakers." Anti-establishment, anti-authoritarian attitudes will likely prevail, and conferences will take on a flavor of activism infrequently encountered in the past. They already have.

As the young adult moves from the campus to the work world, he brings with him a sophistication born of activist rebellion and an acquaintance with principles of behavioral science which promote translating ideas and feelings into behavior. This trend is clearly observable in present conferences.

During the Christmas holidays of 1969, thousands of students devoted several days of their vacation to attend conferences which dealt with racial issues, environmental problems, and population planning. There seemed to be a change in the focus of student interest from the violent rebelliousness of the previous few years to a more thoughtful participative approach to social problems. However, one meeting in Chicago revealed that the feeling of protest was still markedly present. At the conclusion of an address by a government representative, a young student stood up, presumably to ask a question. He used his time at the microphone to ask a series of rhetorical questions: "Why haven't I been able to use the Chicago beaches for the last five years?" "Is Lake Michigan going to go the way of Lake Erie?"

The government representative tried to interrupt in order to respond, but the student refused to let him. Instead he concluded his remarks to the effect that government was impotent and double-dealing and that he intended to have no part in a conference that promised only to give more lipservice to the problem. He walked out, followed by a large number who evidently sympathized with his point of view. (It should be added that another student quickly took the mike, stated that breaking off dialogue was poor problem-solving technique, proceeded to carry on with his questions, and the conference continued.)

The most successful conferences of the 70s will break away, creatively, from the old patterns. At one unique conference on environmental problems, called the Great Grey Ice Gathering, booths were set up in an arena for the distribution of information and literature. The schedule was loose and continuous. People could come and go. During the afternoon about 500 students and young people dropped by. On stage, rock groups pounded out music to a variegated group of young people sitting on the basketball court. Between numbers, scientists and government speakers made their pitches. After the speeches one of the young women (a cochairman of the conference) exclaimed, "It's terrible! Terrible! I agree with everything he said. But you've got to shout and scream if you want to involve people." Her cochairman, a graduate student, complained, "They were too dressed up. They looked like the Establishment."

So the second half of the program was revised. The speakers came down from the stage and stood among the students, who gathered in semicircles on the basketball court and fired point-blank questions at them. The cochairman was cheerful. "This is what it should have been in the beginning," she said. "It's great!"

Given the temporariness of subcultures and their beliefs, it is not difficult to understand the sense of play which permeates the activities of the young. Even when dealing with the most serious of topics they desire immediacy, a shortcircuiting of cognition in order to achieve an immersion at the level of feelings. To be "with it," to sense "where it is," or, in the Heinlein sense (it used to be called a peak experience) to "grok" or achieve a full understanding throughout your being, is a highly sought-after goal.

Only then is a thing experienced as real. Up to that point, young people play at being adults. The entertaining aspect of modern conference designs serves very real purposes in providing fun, in contrast to learning through the hard, dull processes formerly considered necessary, and at the same time reaching the participant through feelings and emotions. Such paths are much more affecting and enduring than the intellect alone. At the environmental conference, for instance, the keynote address was scrapped in favor of another method of gaining a quick involvement during the first session. The participants were seated in several circles. A large box in the center of each circle was papered on each side with photographs of poignant, challenging, or even disgusting pollution problems. The conference began in silence. The participants were asked to try to feel themselves a part of one of the pictures and to talk about it when ready. The silence gradually turned to a hubbub of conversation. The conference was off to a flying start. There was no need for a speaker to remind them of why they were there, to arouse their concern, to produce statistics, nor to provide verbal sticks and carrots. Their existing feelings and the photographic stimulus supplied immediacy and motivation. More important, they felt it was "for real." The problem to which the conference was addressed became theirs in a way that exhortation could probably not have accomplished.

There is a seduction in the "happening" way of life which is very appealing. The Great Grey Ice Gathering promised to be fun because it began differently and promised to be important because feelings were immediately engaged. During the next decade we will find an ever fewer number of conference participants who have not had some experience with laboratory training or encounter groups. These group experiences set a very high standard of involvement, of personal learning, and of satisfaction against which every other group experience will be measured. Subsequent experiences, such as topical conferences, will succeed as they provide equally involving, rewarding, and meaningful designs. Conferences, in brief, will tend to be only cne stage in a continuing process of defining areas of concern, problem-solving, action planning, and implementation. Liberated education is seeking wisdom, not information. The newer conferences may be much less self-conscious in their format, less serving of the status needs of experts, less bound to a time schedule, and always more open to follow newly emerging concepts which result from individuals and groups providing cross-stimulation. We will be less sure of what is and more concerned with what might be.

We are already learning that the teacher-student contract must be renegotiated. It is mistaken to be objective, for instance, about subjective topics like philosophy, religion, love, people, politics, and much of the substance of the social sciences. The student spontaneously pursues knowledge when he is a part of the subject matter. Even in the more objective sciences, there are occasionally techniques for capitalizing on the self-motivating value of personal involvement. A geography teacher, for instance, trying to make his subject matter come alive for a class of slow-learning high school students, had them construct an imaginary country, complete with cities, mountains, rivers and ports, plains and forests. Then each class member became an element of the country and had to be ready to react appropriately as the teacher fed national problems to the group. They dealt with a flood of immigrants, a hurricane, a newly opened foreign market for wheat, and a population explosion. The students worked so hard to be ready to interact appropriately that they haunted the library, questioned their parents, visited government offices, and in general created a model of learning that became the envy of the class for the gifted next door.

At other levels we are seeing college classes in law challenging long-established precedents by pursuing real consumer problems into the courts; free universities where anyone teaches his thing to any others who want to learn. Self-help centers are developing to replace some of the legalistic establishment offices, and both urban and rural communes are experimenting with a new and more satisfying way of life.

In the past years, while change has been rapid, not all of it has touched each of us as individuals. Like the scales on a fish, our participation in modernity forms an overlapping pattern. Identifications with our parents have imbedded in us certain traditional convictions. We have developed a few of our own and from our children adopted a few which we regard as avant garde. But we have accommodated to what we regard as real and possible. We have, without realizing it, accepted an institutionalization of hypocrisy which is the gap between our fondest principles and our usual ability or willingness to stick our necks out by putting them into practice. In a time of rapid change, however, or when the different age groups come into contact, institutionalization of hypocrisy tends to break down. Everyone searches for a firm middle ground where the exceptions to dearly held values are defined. The gaps between principles and practice appear without disguise. As Kenneth Keniston has pointed out, one of the central characteristics of today's youth is that "they insist on taking seriously a great variety of political, personal, and social principles that 'no one in his right mind' ever before thought of attempting to extend to such situations as dealing with strangers, relations between the races, or international politics. For example, peaceable openness has long been a creedal virtue in our society, but it has rarely been extended to foreigners, particularly those with dark skins. Similarly, equality has long been preached, but the American dilemma has been resolved by a series of institutionalized hypocrisies that exempted Negroes from the application of this principle. Love has always been a formal value in Christian societies, but really to love one's enemies—to be generous to policemen, customers, criminals, servants, or foreigners—has been considered folly." [1]

The conference planner of the next decade will need to be constantly checking his own assumptions and values in order to uncover discrepancies between principle and practice. We are very often unaware of our own hypocrisy. Thus, the conference planner will be more successful as he checks whether he is adhering to form or demonstrating substance in his behavior. Does he really believe in planning with a substantial body of the prospective participants? Is he manipulative, getting some Machiavellian glee from an exercise or activities where the end point is invisible to those embroiled in the process? Can he be sufficiently flexible to turn about-face in the light of emerging attitudes or events, or to throw out a carefully prepared program? Can we only function in one kind of order, or can we see that several alternative ways of learning, planning, interacting may be equally beneficial?

It is not easy to give up one's cherished shibboleths. While watching the Broadway production of "Hair," I felt my temperature rise as the actors fooled around with the American flag. They tossed it, dragged it, wrapped it around one another, and it was only when they began to fold it in what I saw was the proper, correct way that I felt a sense of relief. In the middle of the folding ritual, one of the actors turned to the audience and said, "If you fold the flag properly, that is respecting your country." Only then did I perceive what the entire play was about, and through that I gained some additional insight into the young adult of today. It is not form but substance that we must be concerned about. It is not ritual but reality which will make a difference. And too often we do not recognize which is which.

The conference planner and manager who is seen as authentic will receive optimal cooperation from the young adult participant. But he is in trouble if he unquestioningly adheres to old designs or the "conference method." The relationship between conference planners and participants during the 70s will best follow the model of the new understanding between teacher and pupil. Openness is coming easier to the young. They are increasingly able to speak for themselves and to reveal feelings unabashed. They stand unawed by authority. The act of rebellion is in part an

---

[1] Keniston, Kenneth. "The Burden of Violence." *Adolescence for Adults.*

assertion of the ability to rebel. The teacher (planner) who would establish his credentials must be equally open, must be someone in his own right (not a mouthpiece of creed), someone who merits attention from others. He must listen as much as speak, and must be free to feel along with others. He will probably not be a central figure during the conference itself. He will perform a consultant role, monitoring for developing reactions, resourceful in suggesting means of capitalizing on emerging issues. He will be useful in crisis and ingenious in gathering evaluation data. He will be free and help others to be equally so. We need new conference models for the years ahead. Can we do better than strive to be creative and authentic?

Building the
Conference Community

KENNETH D. BENNE and
CHARLOTTE K. DEMOREST

A person who goes to a conference has to travel in two senses. We are all aware of the GECGRAPHICAL TRAVEL *required. Problems with travel budgets, personal or organizational, would not let us forget it, even if we wanted to. Less apparent—but more important from the standpoint of what the participants gain from the experience—is the* SOCIAL TRAVEL *involved. Every conference is a miniature society which is set up to assimilate, for the time, immigrants from various back-home cultures. Its aim is to produce changes in these immigrants through conference associations—changes which will modify, directly or indirectly, back-home practices and patterns. This article is an analysis of the problem of building a conference community which supports rather than thwarts conference purposes.*

The Conference Island

The person who attends a conference is both an emigrant and an immigrant. He emigrates for the time from the familiar continent of his work setting, his everyday organizational involvements, his home, and his neighborhood. He immigrates into an island culture deliberately set up with certain aims and objectives in mind. He comes under the influence, at least potentially, of people who are different from those with whom he ordinarily associates. He enters into relation-

Reprinted by special permission of ADULT LEADERSHIP, of the Adult Education Association of the United States, and of the authors.

ships with people whose back-home reality differs from his
own. He lives in a set of social arrangements, by a set of
standards and mores which are different, at least in some
respects, from those to which he is accustomed. He travels
into a new culture which is designed to make him different
at the end from the way he was when he came.

When we stop to think of it, this travel into a new culture
is essential in providing opportunities for change and growth
for the people attending the conference. But it does raise
problems for the participant about how he is to handle the
differences between the conference reality (the here and
now) and the home reality (the there and then). The society
of the conference needs to be different enough to challenge
the customary ways and beliefs of the participants. However,
it must not be so out of this world that participants can build
no bridges in thought and action between what takes place in
the conference and what goes on back home.

Just as being a member of two societies presents important
problems of adjustment for the conference participant, so
does it present a problem for those who assume responsibilities in setting up the conference. How can they help to build
the kind of conference community which supports each participant in solving constructively his problems of dual membership?

No Conference Community—No Effect

One thing is certain. Unless the immigrants become genuine
members of the conference society—participants in its life,
its play, and its work—the experience will have little, if any,
lasting effect on them. There must be built into the conference
a community in which immigrants can have and feel membership. Otherwise, they remain tourists in the conference
culture. They may take home interesting gadgets from a
strange and far-off land. They may take home gossip, kindly
or malicious, about the ways of the great and the lowly
encountered in the "cloud-cuckoo" land of the conference.
They may take home wise sayings from the head men of the
tribe who spoke to them there on ceremonial occasions. They
may take back tales to regale the home folks between jobs,
when nothing *important* needs to be done. But they will take
back no genuine alternatives for thinking and doing to challenge and to improve the customary ways of their tribe back
home.

Ways of Handling Dual Membership

There are three typical ways in which the participant can handle the problem of his dual membership in a conference and a home community. How he handles the problem during the conference will have a lot to do with what he does, if anything, with his conference experience when he goes home.

The first way has already been suggested: the *tourist* reaction. The traveler, resisting involvement in the conference culture, strives to maintain psychological distance from the groups and people there who might influence him to change. His rejection may be motivated by fear that new ideas—new challenges—might undermine the comfort and security of his position in his back-home environment. He may resent assuming the role of learner from others, as being beneath the dignity of a person of his importance in the organization where he lives and works. Or he may distrust the conference leadership. Whatever the source of his motives to avoid full participation, he seeks in a variety of ways to minimize possible influences on his habitual ways of thinking, evaluating, and acting. He may reject the different ideas of others as being "theoretical" and "impractical." He may reject the methods of the conference as being unlike the way things operate at home and, therefore, as being inapplicable there. He may overemphasize the uniqueness of his own situation and its demands, which means, of course, that experience in or from other situations cannot fit his own. And he may find reinforcement from cronies among the conference membership who feel, with him, that the conference experience has little or nothing in it for them except as it reinforces their present ideas and practices and reassures them that they do not need to change.

The second type of reaction may be called the *expatriate* reaction. Far from rejecting the conference experience, the expatriate accepts it enthusiastically and uncritically. What he rejects, at least for the time, is his back-home situation and membership. Reality for him comes to be the conference. He is starry-eyed about conference ideas and methods. He deprecates the benighted ways of back home and vows, publicly or privately or both, to go back home and change the thinking and the practices there to the conference image. His motives, like those of the tourist, may be various. He may feel deeply dissatisfied with his position back home, and he may see the prestige of having attended the conference as a tool in improving that position. He may feel isolated at home and respond to the acceptance and comradeship he finds at the conference. The conference may tap his idealism in one way or another and develop the latent missionary in him. Whatever the motives, the results are easy to predict. The conference experience will probably lead to increased isolation of the expatriate when he goes back home. He may attempt to apply conference ideas and practices wholesale to the job situation or to the home organization. He increases resistance on the part of others who were not at the conference and resent attempted changes based on experiences that they have not had. The participant, bruised by rebuffs from the home folks, may continue to rebel or may develop a cynical resignation toward the benightedness of those with whom he must work.

The adjustment which promises most intelligent carry-over of conference outcomes to the world outside differs psychologically from both the tourist and the expatriate reactions. We might call it the *learner* reaction. The learner recognizes and accepts the fact of dual membership and of the discrepancies and conflicts between his two sets of loyalties and demands. He accepts membership in the conference community and opens himself to influence from others who are there. But he does not accept these influences uncritically. He tests conference ideas against back-home problems and situations. He relates relevant back-home experiences to the problems discussed at the conference. He faces realistically the problem of transferring conference learnings and recommendations and applying them in the back-home culture to which he will return after the conference has disbanded.

Building a Conference Which Supports the Learner Reaction

If the third pattern of adjustment promises more carry-over of conference effects into the world outside, how can conference arrangements be designed to support this adjustment in the participants? How can wholehearted participation in conference life be encouraged and, at the same time, responsibility for relating conference experiences to back-home realities be developed and maintained? These questions cannot be successfully answered by any one meeting or session of the conference, whether at the beginning or at the end. If they are to be well answered, they must be kept in mind at every stage of conference planning. In fact, finding answers includes preconference preparation and postconference follow-up, as well as what is done at the conference itself.

There are five principal steps that can be taken to induce conference participants to behave more like thoughtful learners and less like tourists or expatriates.

1. *The conference can set a standard of active responsibility on the part of all participants for determining the goals of the conference and for working to achieve them.*

A conference-planning committee should begin to work against the tourist reaction in its earliest preconference communications with participants. When the committee asks prospective participants by mail to list problems and themes for the conference or to react to and supplement a list which it has prepared, it is helping to establish this standard. It is saying, in effect, that every member of the conference community is expected to contribute, that the emphases and goals of the conference are for all participants to determine, not for the planning committee alone.

When the planning committee asks participants to spend a large amount of conference time in groups small enough so that all can contribute to conference thinking and conclusions, it is reinforcing this standard.

Whether this standard of active, responsible membership in the conference comes to have meaning for the individual participant depends in part on what small group he decides he wants to work in. The briefing he is given about making this choice, whether by mail before the conference or at an early orientation session, should reflect this standard. Each participant is asked, first of all, to consider the choice seriously, to think of his responsibilities to the conference in making the choice. In choosing his group he is asked to assess his own needs for learning. But he is asked also to choose a group in which he can make a contribution out of his own experience to the thinking and learning of others.

Finally, this standard of active, responsible membership is reinforced by suggesting to each participant that he make suitable preparation for the conference. His preparation may take the form of studying and thinking about the problem with which his conference group will deal, as it appears in his home setting. He may be asked to prepare by trying out his ideas about the problem on his home associates and getting their reactions to it. He may be asked to prepare by studying working papers which have been distributed before the conference or by doing other relevant reading. But whatever the form of the preparation, the implication is that membership in the conference means responsibility to help make the conference as effective as possible.

2. *The conference can accept a standard that all participants are responsible not only to themselves and to other conference members but to their associates in the home setting as well.*

As the first standard was designed to make it difficult for any member to become a tourist, the second is aimed to make it difficult for him to fall into the expatriate reaction. It means, in effect, that the learning and thinking he is doing at the conference is not an end in itself, but a means of helping him to work with the home folks in dealing more effectively with their problems.

Here again, a planning committee can begin to set this standard in preconference communications to participants. When the committee asks for suggestions of problems and themes for the conference, it can encourage each participant to consult his colleagues before sending in his reply.

The community can go one step behind this procedure and encourage organizations and agencies concerned to spend time in selecting the appropriate participants to send to the conference. The organizations can be asked to use criteria of organizational need as well as individual need in selecting conference participants. Recognizing that carry-over of conference learnings into the home situation is likely to be much greater if more than one local person attends the conference, the committee can encourage organizations to instruct and send teams of participants rather than individuals. It is true that rigid instructions to participants regarding what they are expected to bring home can operate to prevent them from both entering wholeheartedly into what develops at the conference and learning from it. But it is equally true that if the home folks have no expectation that the participants who are going to the conference will bring back help, the participants are less likely to take the conference experience seriously. If, however, they are seriously concerned, and if they go home with new attitudes, ideas, or skills, they are likely to find themselves alienated from their back-home associates. Probably the planning committee's best approach is to encourage agencies and organizations to select and instruct teams of participants, but to suggest, at the same time, realistic criteria of selection and briefing. The committee can support the idea that the best things participants can take home are not answers to specific problems, but new tools for diagnosing those problems and new ways of working toward solutions.

At the conference, participants can be discouraged from an uncritical acceptance of ideas, whether these ideas come from resource persons or from other participants. A premium can be put upon contributions directed toward testing and criticizing proposals and reported experiences, provided these follow upon, rather than precede, an honest attempt to understand what the proposals mean. If a participant can test conference ideas in terms of their application to back-home realities, he will remain loyal to his back-home responsibilities as he participates in the community of the conference.

Finally, time can be left in the conference schedule for teams of participants to meet from time to time to relate, as they develop, their conference experiences to back-home problems. There are advantages in having members of a team from the same home base assigned to different work groups. But there are advantages also in having teams meet as teams during the conference to compare and interrelate varying experiences. Such meetings will make it more difficult for individuals to develop and consistently maintain either an expatriate or tourist attitude toward the conference.

3. *The conference can prepare resource persons to help to keep conference deliberations geared to the back-home realities of participants.*

Resource persons are always tempted to use their expertness and status to impress other participants with their unusual wisdom and competence. A parade of virtuosity, unrelated to the problems of participants, may impress and entertain them; but it is unlikely to leave much learning or commitment that will make differences in the conduct of participants when they once more face their home problems directly. Such use of resources, by burning bridges of perceived connection between conference reality and back-home reality, may foster either tourist or expatriate reactions in the participants, depending on which reality is more attractive to them.

The alternative is to prepare resource persons (and materials, also) to relate available sources of knowledge and experience from other settings to the back-home problems of the participants. The resource person is encouraged to act as a consultant to the participants, either in a work group or in individual interviews. His effort is not to peddle answers to difficulties and problems, but to help participants see their problems more clearly, more comprehensively, more deeply than they did before.

Four conditions encourage this kind of resource use: (a) Resource persons who are willing and able to work in consultative relations to participants are selected. (b) Resource persons are briefed on the purposes of the conference and the problems that participants are bringing with them. (c) Participants are told in an early session about the ways in which the resource persons expect to be used. (d) Some directory of available resources is made available to participants, so that each can plan a schedule of consultation within conference limits of time and availability.

4. *The conference can dramatize and clarify the problems of applying conference outcomes to the world outside.*

When any learner in one situation tries to apply what he has learned in another situation, he runs into problems. The participant who makes a wholesale transfer of conference methods or recommendations to a back-home situation that is different, in important respects, from the conference situation is inviting a wholesale rejection of these methods and recommendations if they do not, by accident, work out well. He may reject them himself if they prove unsuccessful, and his colleagues in the home situation are almost certain to do so. On the other hand, if he overstresses differences between the conference situation and the back-home setting, while neglecting the features common to both, he may make it hard for himself or others to try *any* transfer of conference outcomes.

At some conferences, a general session is devoted specifically to the problem of applying principles and recommendations. Individuals or teams may report on postconference plans. Experts or participants or both may then make a clinical critique of these plans. Or participants may be asked to act out their projected first step after arriving home, whether this step is reporting to the boss, discussing the conference at a staff meeting, or trying out some new technique in the job setting. The other participants can then discuss what has been acted out and can clarify and face the problems involved in returning home after their week-end spree on the conference island.

5. *The conference can discourage emphasis on irrelevant outside ranks or positions and can encourage the development of a status system in the conference which supports rather than thwarts conference objectives.*

All of us have seen work groups and conferences hampered and inhibited by the carrying-over of big shot-little shot, boss-employee, teacher-pupil relationships from the outside world into the conference society. The big shots may occupy most of the time of the work groups by talking, whether their ideas merit the time or not. The little shots may hesitate to challenge the big shots—either their ideas or their monopolization of time—even though the little shots may have insights, ideas, and experience more relevant to the problems being discussed and better thought through and expressed. Similarly, the employee hesitates to challenge the boss, and the pupil hesitates to challenge the teacher, even when the learning and growth of the group or of the individual require the challenge.

One way in which the problem can be handled is to put the big shots in one work group, the little shots in another. But this kind of grouping usually does not follow the patterns which either the needs of the individuals or the needs of the organization represented would suggest. The more rational bases of grouping normally demand that people of different social status in the outside world work and think together.

There is only one fundamental way of handling the problem: Develop a standard, in the conference community and in its constituent groups, that contributions are to be evaluated and rewarded not on the basis of who made them, but on the basis of how well they contribute to the clarification and solution of the problems being discussed. Where this standard prevails, Instructor A can talk up to Dean B when he feels the Dean's ideas are irrelevant or otherwise faulty, without fear and with approval from others as well as the Dean. Or Housewife X can show the inapplicability of Family Expert Y's ideas, with general rejoicing all around.

It is no easy task for a group or a conference community to

develop such a standard of behavior. The planning committee or the group leader cannot legislate it. It must grow out of the attitudes and expectations of the members if it is to be effective. But the planning committee and designated leaders can help to build such a standard at points where irrelevant outside status is most likely to be smuggled in. What are some of these most common points of illegal entry where the conference community needs to be fortified?

One point is the use of names and titles in the conference. The title, "Doctor Zilch," on a name tag (or in his self-introduction to his group or in remarks to or about him by a chairman) may release attitudes of awe and self-censorship in "Mrs. Mouseman," another group member, which render her quite incapable of free interaction with Dr. Zilch and his ideas. And Dr. Zilch may have a self-image of Mahatma Zilch so reinforced by public recognition of his academic burden that he finds it difficult to do anything but pontificate in the group. Names without titles on the name tags worn by participants may help to discourage the parading of titles as status labels. Sometimes, in conferences where the practice does not seem an affectation to the members, the use of first names is encouraged, following the long-established practice of the Society of Friends, who have tried in this way to keep unmerited status out of their association.

In addition to titles, self-introductions in small work groups offer a temptation to the status-conscious. Early in the conference, when participants do not know where they stand in relation to others, there are pressures on every participant to use self-introduction as an opportunity to build himself up with his new and unknown associates. He may do this by telling of all his important offices and experiences, whether they are relevant to the group task or not. Although there is nothing inherently wrong with a person's building himself up when he needs a build-up, such extraneous material adds little knowledge or experience to the progress of group discussion. It may even provoke unproductive competition among group members.

Some work-group leaders try to meet this problem by suggesting simple introductions in the opening session of the group—perhaps name, work, and home location. Sometimes they discourage initial introductions completely, feeling that the best way for people to get acquainted with one another is for them to start working on problems of common concern.

There is often an advantage in a group's knowing what the areas of special competence of its members are, so that the group will know where to turn when special resources are needed. When this is true, the aim is to get clear, self-objective statements from the members, limited to information which seems at the time to be useful to the group. The same rule applies to introductions of special resource persons or of speakers in large sessions or in small work groups. The status established by such introductions is functional in furthering the work of the conference.

As conference planners examine established conference arrangements and rituals, they may discover supports to status relations which thwart rather than serve the objectives of a democratic conference community. Does the conference staff have different and better housing than the participants? Is there a reason for these distinctions? Are staff and resource persons separated from participants at meals or during social occasions? If so, why? Do people with no function in the program sit on the stage at general sessions? What effects does this have on conference attitudes? Such questions must be faced and answered by a planning committee that seeks to exclude irrelevant status from the conference community.

The Conference Planners' Task

Like all educational arrangements, a conference builds a temporary association designed to produce changes in people who become members of it. It encounters a danger common to all educational arrangements—the danger of isolation from the realities of the surrounding society which ideally it is designed to alter and improve. Life in an educational community—in this case, the conference—always raises for the learner problems of adjustment to dual-group memberships. The task for conference planners is to design supports to healthy, rather than unproductive, solutions to these problems.

Program Development

RICHARD BECKHARD

In the initial planning of a conference or workshop, a tentative program is developed, based on the objectives to be reached, suggestions from the organization leadership and some of the membership or participants, and past experience with similar meetings.

The job of program planners is to take all these ideas and try to design a program that will effectively move toward the organization or program goals and will provide optimum opportunities for participation, sharing of experience, and use of the resources within the group.

Form of the Meeting

There is usually one form of meeting that can best be adapted to particular purposes or objectives. Following is a list of the principal types of meetings and their characteristics. For each meeting that is planned, one of these is probably especially appropriate:

Type	Usually Used for	Characteristics
Convention	Annual meetings	General sessions and committee meetings, mostly information giving and voting on official business. May use subgroups within general session
Work conference	Planning, fact finding, or problem solving	General sessions and face-to-face groups; high participation

Reprinted from HOW TO PLAN AND CONDUCT WORKSHOPS AND CONFERENCES by Richard Beckhard, by special permission of Association Press and of the author.

Type	Usually Used for	Characteristics
Institute	Training	General sessions, some face-to-face groups; staff provides most resources
Workshop	Training	General sessions and face-to-face groups; participants are resources
Seminar	Group of experienced people, or resources share experience	High participation, usually face-to-face groups; leader is discussion leader, not only content expert
Clinic	Clinical exploration of some particular subject; usually participants in trainee role, clinic leaders in training role	Usually face-to-face, but may be general sessions and face-to-face

In addition to these complex types (those with more than one kind of grouping), there are several kinds of small-group meetings with which planners are likely to be concerned. Most staff, board, and committee meetings fall into the small-group category, as do many training workshops. The same planning principles apply equally to the various types, although the conducting problems and leadership methods in the small-group meetings may be quite different from those in multiple-group meetings.

It may be helpful to identify briefly some of the more frequently used types of *small conferences: problem-solving* (for exploring problems, making policy, making decisions); *information-giving* (mostly one-way communication—may be practical for part of a staff meeting or training meeting); *information-* or *opinion-exchanging* (experience-sharing); *fact-finding* or *exploratory* (for collecting information on issues—extremely useful for assessing needs).

Groupings Commonly Used in Workshops, Conferences, and Institutes

As each type of meeting has a variety of possible groupings, specific decisions on how to handle each part of the meeting must be made.

Grouping	*Kinds of Subject Matter*	*Group or Number of Participants*
General sessions	Information giving Orientation Reporting to total group Voting Business meetings Demonstrations Speeches, lectures	Total conference group
Plenary sessions	General session with official action (business meeting, delegate assembly, and others)	Total official group (voting members)
Work groups	Working on a problem or aspect of a problem, to come up with action, recommendation, or finding; report usually expected; may meet once or several times	Usually not more than 10-20, to allow maximum participation; group composed heterogeneously from conference groups
Special-interest groups	Composed around common interests of members in a problem or back-home job; exchange of opinions, experiences, ideas; usually no action required, although findings may be produced	10-20, to allow for maximum participation
Occupational groups	Special-interest groups, built around back-home jobs of members	Determined by number in same occupation
Application groups	Designed to apply new learnings or information to other situations of the members	7-15
Skill-practice groups	Found in workshops and institutes, designed to give members practice opportunities in subject being studied (leadership training, conference leadership)	12-18

		Group or Number
Grouping	Kinds of Subject Matter	of Participants
Training groups or process groups	Specialized form used in some human relations workshops, where subject is study of group process and group behavior	12-20
Off-the-record groups	Small groups designed to give participants opportunities to react to the conference; no reporting required, but may become informal channel to conference staff for gripes, suggestions; an official conference bull session	5-10
Orientation groups	Small groups that meet once at beginning of conference for introduction and orientation	5-10

Nature of Material To Be Presented in Determining Groupings

Certain kinds of subjects, such as new information; resolutions; and new theories, policies, and principles obviously can be more effective if handled in a presentation before the *total group* than through any other type of grouping. Official actions, such as voting, action on committee reports, and the like, are also obviously *general-session* topics. Key personalities or featured speakers fall easily into *general-session* meetings.

However, when the material to be covered involves recommendations for a future course of action or possible ways of handling a complex problem, it must be decided whether this can best be handled in one session with the total group or explored in small groups where more people can take part in the deliberations.

Assuming that the decision is to use small groups, what factors determine whether *work groups* or *special-interest groups* are more appropriate? Here again, the nature of the material can be helpful. For instance, if independent reactions of teachers and parents on some problem at a PTA meeting are desirable, it would be wise to use *special-interest groups;* if, however, we wish to have teachers and parents share their points of view in small groups in order to arrive at some common agreements, *work groups* should probably be used. Each session of a conference needs to be analyzed in this way, with attention to the kinds of material to be presented.

The Situation in Which the Material Is To Be Presented

Following the decision on the kind of material to be presented, probably the next step should be to analyze the situation in which it is to be presented. For example, a keynote speech delivered first on a program, before the participants are ready to listen, can seriously impair the effectiveness of a conference. Similarly, a summary given at the end of a long, hard day may fall on deaf ears. It is important to think about the audience's attitude toward each subject, the fatigue factor, the relationship to other subjects on the program, the kinds of resources needed, and the methods chosen.

Here are several questions, the answers to which should provide some guidance in program scheduling:

Where will this subject best fit into the program—morning? Afternoon?

How interested is the audience in this subject?

How important is this subject to the organization? to the audience?

How does it tie in with the objectives of the meeting?

How familiar is the audience with this subject (for example, the annual history of the organization given for new members)?

What are audience attitudes toward the subject? (Is this a "hot," controversial subject?)

How much participation is anticipated?

Would this be better handled in the total group or in small groups? Why?

If in small groups, should the groups be composed of individuals from similar back-home situations or should each group be mixed to include different backgrounds? Why?

What kinds of program resources will be necessary for this subject? in general sessions? in small groups?

Methods of Presentation

After deciding what material will be handled in what kind of grouping, the question of how to present the material has to be faced. The problem in small face-to-face groups is one of determining how much information the chairman or special resources should give in relation to time spent in discussion by the participants. The problem in the large general-session meeting is to determine which of several large-meeting presentation methods will be most effective. Again the criteria applied can be the *nature of the material* and the *situation in which it is being presented.* There is no one *right* way to present any subject, but most large-meeting presentations fall into the following categories, and the choice, therefore, is to determine which of them will best achieve the specific objectives:

Speaker (unassisted, no visual aids)	Most appropriate for lecture, personal experience — inspirational — information giving
Speaker with visuals	Describing technical subject—training —discussing complex subject—dealing with controversial matter
Demonstration	Demonstrating things, processes, a procedure
Situation demonstration	Demonstrating behavior (for example, leading a discussion, handling an interview)
Dramatic action	A skit or stunt designed to drive home a point of view
Panel, symposium, debate, or forum	Presentation of different points of view on a subject. Panel has interaction among members. In symposium, each person talks to or through chairman
Films or television	

Audience Participation

Providing adequate opportunities for participation is a prime requirement of successful conference planning. Today's conference goer or workshop participant not only wants, but expects, such opportunities. One way has been mentioned— through the subdivision of the total group into small working groups where everyone has a chance to take part. Leaders of such groups need to be skilled in discussion leadership, so that they can encourage and stimulate participation by all members of the group. Discussed below are a few tested ways of involving the audience in the large *general-session* group.

QUESTIONS AND QUESTION PERIODS

Question periods, frequently used but also frequently misused, sometimes fail to accomplish their objectives because of poor scheduling—inadequate time allowed or placed at the wrong spot in the program. Or perhaps the audience has not been properly prepared to ask questions. A speaker, finishing his lecture, asks, "Are there any questions?" The only questions may be those which relate to the last part of the speech, since there is no time for the audience to think back to its earlier parts. Many good questions never get asked because questioners are too shy to ask them in so large a group. Then, too, the questions may not have been screened for relevance. A well-organized presentation of ideas can be ruined by a disorganized discussion during the question period.

Some general rules for question periods may be useful. Questions should be crystallized while they are "hot"—written down during the presentation. Too, if people know in advance that they are expected to ask questions, they will listen better. Arrangements for someone to screen the questions—organize them into categories and combine similar ones into one general question—will help the speaker to give his answers in a more logical, systematic way. Those who are to answer questions will want to keep the audience-member point of view in mind. People ask questions because (a) they need clarification or amplification of a point; (b) they do not see the application to their own situation; (c) they disagree with a point made; (d) they are trying to broaden the point to cover other situations. If planners think of question periods as an important part of the program, not merely as an appendage, they will schedule adequate time, will locate them where they are most pertinent in the schedule, and will devise methods for handling them effectively.

BUZZ GROUPS

"Buzz group" is the term applied to the division of an audience into groups of 6-10 persons to get wide participation quickly on a very limited subject. The audience members turn their chairs to form small circles; or three or four persons in the first row turn around and face the same number directly behind them in the second row, the third row faces the fourth row, and so on.

The *buzz group is particularly useful* (a) to give everyone a chance to react to a speech or presentation and to discuss its application; (b) to sample audience opinion relative to an issue or to a decision to be made; (c) to enable the members to share their common experiences in some practice or problem; (d) to give everyone a chance to express an opinion on a subject to a group of colleagues.

Buzz groups sometimes fail because they are used inappropriately. Some of the common reasons for failure are these: (a) the task, the procedure, the machinery, or the instructions were not clear to the participants; (b) the task was too complex for a buzz group of 10 or 15 minutes' duration.

Tell the audience what roles are needed. Usually the buzz groups will not need a chairman or even a convener, but they may need a recorder to synthesize the discussion and report back to the group. They are told that they will have 5 (or 10 or 15) minutes, that they will be given a 2-minute warning before their report must be turned in.

Make sure that everyone is "on the track" by having either the meeting chairman or an assistant or two wander around during the buzz sessions to clarify procedure if necessary.

PHILLIPS 66

Originally developed by J. Donald Phillips at Michigan State College,* "Phillips 66," a form of small group, has a fixed procedure in which three persons from each row face one another to form groups of six. Then they are given six minutes to confer—to decide on a question or give an opinion.

LISTENING TEAMS

The audience is divided into two or three "listening sections" prior to the presentation. The chairman asks each section to listen to the presentation from a particular point of view. For example, the setting is a PTA meeting, and an expert is talking on juvenile delinquency. Perhaps one section listens in terms of what parents can do about the problem; another section, from the point of view of the teacher. After the presentation, the chairman or the speaker calls on several from each listening section or team to report their findings or questions, and the speaker notes or answers them.

Just as is sometimes the case with the buzz groups, the listening-team device may be inappropriate for an occasion because the audience does not feel strongly enough about or know enough about the subject to think in various categories; or the assignment may not be clear; or the speech may have been too thin in content to bear up under a concentrated audience analysis.

---

* Now Michigan State University.

Interview Panel

A panel of audience members representing the various populations in the audience (teachers, parents, college students, and so on) interviews a speaker or a panel of experts, from the point of view of their own group. Such an interview panel may serve to start the question period.

Reaction Panel

A similarly representative group of audience members has the special assignment of asking questions at any time during the speech or presentation. They are to ask questions that they think may be puzzling the group they represent, not their own personal questions.

Observing Teams

Observing teams are similar to listening teams, but are more applicable to training situations. When a situation is being presented, such as conducting a study-group meeting or leading a staff meeting, the audience may be asked to observe the demonstration from several points of view and to report their findings.

Resources—Human and Material

Having determined what subjects are to be covered, where they will be handled (groupings), how material will be presented, and what participation-getting methods will be used, the next step is to determine the resources needed for doing these things. Someone in any or all of the following categories might be needed:

1. Speakers
2. Panel chairmen (for planning presentation as well as for programs)
3. Panel members
4. Content or subject-matter resource persons (for small groups)
5. Discussion leaders
6. Recorders (to record small-group discussions)
7. Reporters (to report discussion—may be combined with recorders)
8. Group observers (where observation of the group's work is desired)

9. Session developers (members who help to create a particular session program or agenda)
10. Unit heads (in large training meetings; examples—co-
ordinator of general sessions, co-ordinator of skill-practice
sessions, work-group co-ordinator)
11. Section chairmen (for special-interest meetings—may
also be discussion leaders)

It will be noted that these are all *program resources*. They do
not include the staff who will handle registration or physical
arrangements or publicity. It is important that planners keep
the two types of functions separated in planning, even though
frequently the same person may be involved in several functions in each category.

Kinds of Planning Help

Some of the program resources are needed during the planning period. The panel chairman, for instance, should be involved in planning the content or agenda and in selecting the
participants on his panel. This not only decentralizes the
planning and spreads responsibility; it also involves more
people in a concern for the outcome of the meeting.

If subgroups are used, leadership teams of discussion leaders, resource persons, recorders, and so on will be needed.
Whenever possible, it is desirable that these people be drawn
from the membership. One way of involving the members in
the planning is to ask them to suggest candidates for such
assignments. Another useful procedure is to select discussion
leaders and ask them to recruit the members of their teams
(resource, recorder).

In the selection of speakers and panel participants, the
membership often can be very valuable. In addition to the help
they can give, the members will feel that they are more closely
a part of the program if they know they have had a part in
selecting the key participants.

Multiple Roles of
the Meeting Planner

GORDON L. LIPPITT

Business and industrial firms, government agencies, schools, and other organizations in our society are placing more and more emphasis on creativity, innovation, and improvement in all kinds of meetings. It has been pointed out that there are 11 million internal meetings held daily by U.S. companies. It has also been established that 13,000 out-of-office meetings were staged in 1967. The cost of internal meetings is estimated at $1 billion annually, and out-of-office meetings, including conventions and trade shows, at $2.5 billion. The pressure for improvement of all these meetings is producing an enlarging role and increased responsibility for skilled meeting planners.

This article attempts to examine the various roles a professional meeting planner is required to perform in meeting the complex needs of his organization, or one to which he is consultant. There are four major roles:

Role No. 1: As a Presentation Specialist
Role No. 2: As a Planner
Role No. 3: As an Information Coordinator
Role No. 4: As a Consultant to Management.

It is my feeling that each of these functions requires somewhat different skills and abilities. In a small organization the meeting planner may perform all four functions, whereas in a larger organization the "head of a department" might well be the consultant to management for planning the meeting while those on his staff design, administer, and conduct the meeting.

Reprinted by special permission of ADULT LEADERSHIP and of the author.

It is probable that the roles of the meeting planner usually emerge in a sequence, as can be seen by reviewing the development of organizational meetings in this country. The earliest meetings were conducted by those who were more or less presentation specialists, recruited because of this particular skill to run sales meetings, new product sessions, or large conventions of organizations. As meetings grew in frequency and importance, the need for better planning became obvious. To ensure the value of meetings, those who worked in business, industry, and government found themselves slowly moving towards the administrative role of planning. As a result, management, in selecting people to direct meetings, discovered it needed good administrators.

In recent years it has been felt that some meeting problems require for their solution a broader attack than that furnished by the usual meeting techniques. This brought into focus the need for the meeting planner also to be an information coordinator. The purpose here was to ensure that meetings were planned on the basis of the communication goals of management. These goals encompassed the information needs of participants, adequate knowledge about the focus of the meeting, and effective information sharing prior to and at the meeting itself to ensure confidence and trust in the meeting process.

At this point, the fourth role—that of contributing to organizational problem solving by being an internal consultant—has emerged.

It is quite likely that the roles of the meeting planner have emerged in this way within most organzations. The emergence of these roles does not mean, however, that the meeting planner has developed the skills necessary to meet the enlarging demands on his function and responsibilities.

Figure 1 illustrates the four roles which we will discuss. It is my feeling that every meeting planner should exercise the initiative to be professionally prepared in *all* four roles and functions.

As A Presentation Specialist

An important aspect here is the ability to use learning theory and effective presentation methods to meet the needs of a particular meeting.

People attending meetings will not be inspired, motivated, changed, or "sold" on an idea or product unless they *learn* something from the experience.

In a recent paper about this need for sophistication about learning, it was stated as follows:

"Since the [meeting planner] is concerned with learning, it follows that he should be concerned with learning theory. [Meeting planners] often talk about the learning theory that underlies their training. However, most of us do not have a good understanding of learning theories and their application to our training efforts."

The behavioral sciences in the last two decades have made major contributions in the area of learning theory, learning methods, and learning skills:

"Research by the behavioral sciences in the learning process is also contributing to the succesful practice of management. Recognizing that people come into a learning situation with an image of themselves as self-directing and responsible persons—not as dependent individuals—is one of the important realities to a superior trying to develop his subordinates. Also we know from behavioral science research that there are different levels of change in the development process. We know that people can increase their knowledge, insight, understanding, skills, attitudes, values, and interests; and we know that different methods are involved in developing different levels of these skills or knowledge."

The responsibility of an enlightened and effective meeting planner is to assure himself that one or more persons engaged in the planning process is knowledgeable in the field of learning principles and practices. This should be a prerequisite for effective meeting designs and, preferably, this knowledge should be held by the meeting planner himself. In addition, of course, he should be knowledgeable about the tools and methods of presentation to implement the goals of the meeting. This will include directing the program, coaching the presentors, selecting correct audiovisual equipment, securing proper facilities, and utilizing the best in human and technical resources. And it goes without saying that the meeting planner should always examine and improve his own presentation skills.

One of the great challenges to the meeting planning function, therefore, is the increased sophistication required in making use of the rapidly growing body of knowledge about how people learn and change, and relating this to the best of presentation methods and resources.

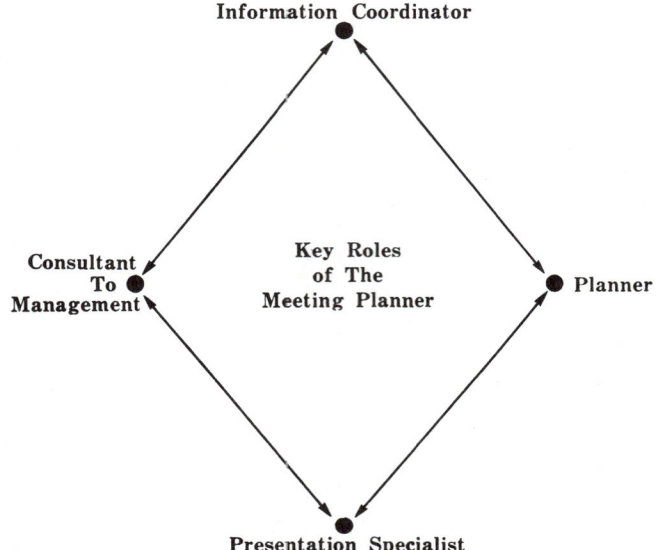

FIGURE 1
Multiple Roles of the Meeting Planner

As A Planner

As organizational meetings proliferated, the administrative
role of planning has begun to demand a major portion of the
meeting planner's time, skill, and energy. In this role he must
apply all the administrative skills. He will need to recruit,
select, and develop his staff team; plan programs; set up the
process of coordination and communication; carry out
financial planning for the meeting; and all of the other
functions of a staff manager:

"The [meeting planner] should know the principles and practices
used in the administration of programs. He should also know the
concepts of management principles, including areas such as
problem solving, the dynamics of organization, controls, and reporting procedures."

But this requirement for managerial skills should not be
frightening:

"There is nothing esoteric or mysterious about planning as such.
It is simply a description of what we want to accomplish in the
future and agreement on the means for achieving it. It is an effort

to arrange for the use of our resources in an orderly, economical, and goal-assuring way."

Dr. Lowell Hattery points out in his monograph, *Planning for Achieving Goals*, that these are the steps in the planning process:

1. Agreeing on and understanding the goals of the organization
2. Gathering information on the nature of the current situation, prospective available resources, and future requirements (forecasting)
3. Involving others in the process
4. Diagnosing needs and setting planning goals
5. Choosing alternative courses of action
6. Agreeing upon responsibility for action
7. Preparing the final plan
8. Getting the plan approved.

The planning function is increasing in importance within large organizational systems, and it is a critical area of skill for the sophisticated meeting planner.

As Information Coordinator

In this function the planner must serve as a seeker of information, clarifier of information, synthesizer of information, reality-tester of information, provider of information, and as a communications "link" in the organization.

Let us examine these functions in more detail:

—As a *seeker* of information the meeting planner must discover the goals and expectations of his organization for the meeting to be planned. He must learn from those sponsoring the meeting what objectives and results are desired and who is to participate. He will want to request certain information from those who will guide the meeting from the platform. He will need to seek out information from those who know about the product to be presented, the program to be sold, the report to be achieved, and whether other input-output information is necessary so that the meeting can serve the proper function. This might by symbolized as follows:

Information Input	Meeting	Information Output
(Planner)		(Implementation)

—As a *clarifier* of information the meeting planner will impart to the involved people the multiplicity of ideas and information he has collected. A meeting in which there is no common understanding of intentions, plans, and objectives is doomed to failure.

—As a *synthesizer* of information the meeting planner will put into a proper frame of reference the different ideas and information which he obtains, bringing it all into focus so that the meeting is not a "hodge podge" of conflicting ideas and parts, but becomes an integrated meeting with a proper sequence of events around a basic theme.

—As a *reality-tester* of information and communication, the meeting planner should always help his superiors, or sponsoring organization, to see that the plans they approve are feasible, workable, and realistic. The desires of management may not always be realistic in light of the allocated budget. The number of persons invited may not make possible the necessary learning goals; the facilities may not accommodate the necessary equipment. A professional meeting planner must assume responsibility for bringing reality into the planning process.

—As a *provider* of information the meeting planner will give proper information and communication to those in the organization from his own experience. He should present ideas, opinions, and concepts that will be helpful in planning a successful meeting. If he cannot do this, he is a "functionnaire," and not a professional member of the management team.

—As a *communications* link in the organization, the meeting planner is the pivot for management, departmental and technical personnel, the meeting presenter, and all others participating in the meeting. Obviously he must be an effective communicator. To be effective he will need to:

- *Be accessible* to those who are working on the meeting or who will participate in it.
- Develop *trust* between himself and all others concerned.
- *Level* with people on plans and problems.
- Keep the *goals* clearly in mind, and help others to do the same.
- *Define* the *responsibilities* of others.
- Develop his *listening skills*.

In this way he will find this not only to be an essential role, but one which is seen as contributing to the greater assurance of a highly successful meeting.

As a Consultant to Management

I come now to the function the author feels is the most important one in the planner's portfolio—serving as a problem-solving consultant.

We have always recognized the need for management to support the meeting planning effort. It is not, however, the support of planning that is the major need. The major need is for meetings to be recognized and used as a valuable tool for management problem solving, which is itself a learning process. The meeting function should serve as an example and a resource to management in the solution of problems.

The new challenge for the meeting planner, then, is to develop his skills and roles in the organization as an internal organizational consultant on problem solving, change, and organizational development. Figure 2 illustrates the way in which this can be accomplished:

1. Helps management examine organizational problems. (*e.g.*: organizes a management meeting for problem identification in the relationships between home and field office personnel.)
2. Helps management examine the contribution of the proper meeting to these problems. (*e.g.*: in relation to home/field office problems, explores with management how a conference on communications might lead to problem solving.)
3. Helps examine the long-range and short-range objectives of the meeting. (*e.g.*: involves management in refining objectives and in setting goals.)
4. Explores, with management, alternatives to meeting plans. (*e.g.*: encourages the examination of the effect of different forms of participative type of meeting, as contrasted with solely a speaker or inspiration approach.)
5. Develops, with management, the meeting plans. (*e.g.*: based on the objectives, works with a steering committee to develop the program, rather than simply submitting an independently developed meeting plan for management for approval.)
6. Explores appropriate resources to implement meeting plan. (*e.g.*: provides management with a variety of resources, both inside and outside the organization. The meeting planner must help management to understand

what each resource can contribute to effective problem solution.)

7. Provides consultation for management on evaluation and review of program. (*e.g.:* evaluation must be in terms of problem solving. Working with management, the meeting planner must make an assessment of the current status of the problem, rather than on whether or not the audience liked the meeting.)

8. Explores with management the follow-up steps necessary to reinforce problem solving and outputs from the meeting. (*e.g.:* encourages management to look at the implications of the steps so far taken, and to assess the current status of the problem in terms of other actions that might now be necessary to follow up on the stimulus of the meeting.)

This "internal consultant" role of the meeting planner is important for the changing organizations of today's society. This role will require increased professionalization and skills in the meeting planner field.

"In a sense everyone is a consultant. Everyone has impulses to give advice, information, or help. Teachers, parents, and friends are consultants. Also, everyone at times feels the need for help. In order that the consultantship between helper and the recipient optimally meets the needs of both parties, appropriate relationships must be built. It is necessary that both parties have certain kinds of skills, knowledge, and awareness in order to establish these relationships."

It is my feeling that more attention needs to be given by management to selecting and developing meeting planners who have the necessary skills. As Richard Beckhard puts it:

"The consultant (or person in a helping role) always enters such a relationship as a person with authority achieved either through position or role in the organization or through the possession of specialized knowledge. To achieve an effective consultative relationship, it is essential that he understand the nature of this power and develop skills to use it in a way which will be viewed as helpful by the person receiving the help.

"A person entering a consulting or helping relationship must have the ability to diagnose the problem and goals of the person being helped, and be able to assess realistically his own motivations for giving the help. He must also recognize the limits of his own resources to help in the particular situation."

FIGURE 2
PROBLEM SOLVING FUNCTION OF THE
MEETING PLANNER

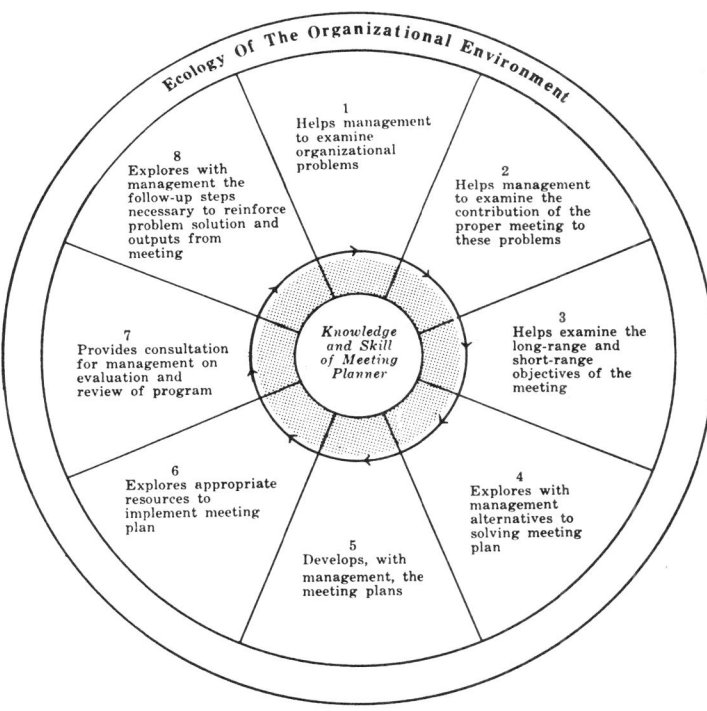

In carrying out a "helping" relationship to management, a meeting planner will find himself operating along the continuum of consulting roles shown in Figure 3. Here I have illustrated some of the major helping relationships from directive to primarily non-directive consultations.

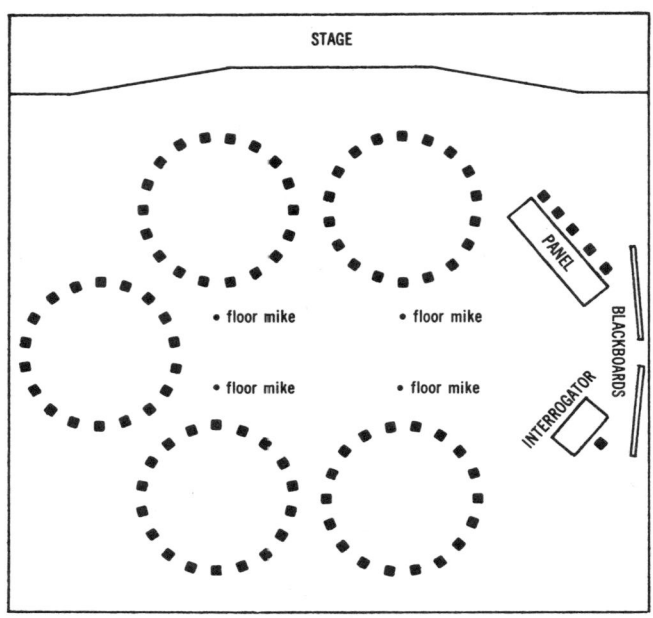

FIGURE 3
Multiple Consulting Approaches of the
Meeting Planner

Position 1: Gives Expert Advice to Management

There will be numerous occasions when management will expect the meeting planner to answer a technical question; for example, a question about the value of a certain kind of meeting and its utilization for the organization.

Position 2: Persuades Management as to a
Proper Approach

In certain circumstances management may be attempting to solve a problem by using a meeting medium or a method which the meeting planner, from his professional experience, feels will not work. The meeting planner may need to use his best persuasive skills, especially if time is short, to persuade management not to use that particular approach.

Position 3: Provides Alternatives to Management

The meeting planner may offer alternatives to management in the solution of a problem. The problem is not one in which he is the implementer of a solution, but one where he recognizes the values of identifying alternatives for management in confronting the learning aspects of a problem and the various kinds of meetings.

Position 4: Assists in Problem-Solving Process

In this situation, the meeting planner serves as a process observer and consultant to management. He does not get involved in the "content" of the problem, which may be outside his area of competence. Rather, he helps management maintain the quality of its meeting and problem-solving planning, through his skill as a specialist in this field.

Position 5: Serves as Catalyst for Management Problem Solving

In this last category, the meeting planner may only ask questions for management to take into account as it considers a certain direction, action, or meeting.

Choice Factors

The choice of which position to take at any given time as a consultant to management is conditioned by these factors:

A. Factors in the meeting planner as a person.
   —Skills as a consultant.
   —Ability to work with others.
   —Experience in the area of the problem.
   —Self-image.
   —Level of knowledge and skill as a meeting specialist.
B. Factors in the relationship between management and the meeting planner.
   —Status in the organization.
   —Previous role in management problem solving.
   —Familiarity with organization history and objectives.
   —Ability to influence management.
   —Previous successes and failures in working with other elements of the organization.
C. Factors in the problem situation.
   —Knowledge of the content of the problem.

—Time available for solution.
—Ability to see alternatives.

The Challenge to the Meeting Planner

In this article, I have tried to present an inclusive view of the multiple roles of the meeting planner. With the greater demand for meetings, increased specialization of meeting designs, and the increased needs of organizations, I feel all these functions are needed. In many cases, management is not aware of the potential help it has available from its meeting planning, resource specialist. It should be said, however, that meeting planners sometimes have not been creative, innovative, or professional enough to see and fulfill all four roles and functions or to develop the skills necessary for their fulfillment.

This is a challenge to all of us who seek to meet the increasing demands placed on the meeting planner by today's organizations.

REFERENCES

Auger, Bert Y., *How to Run an Effective Meeting;* Commerce, October 1967.

Beckhard, Richard, *The Leader Looks at the Consultative Process;* Leadership Resources, Inc. 1961.

Gibb, Jack R., *The Role of the Consultant;* The Journal of Social Issue, Vol. XV, No. 2, 1959.

Hattery, Lowell II, *Planning for Achieving Goals,* Monograph, 1966, Leadership Resources, Inc., Washington, D. C.

Lippitt, Gordon L., *Implications of the Behavioral Sciences for Management;* Public Personnel Review, July 1966.

This, Leslie E. and Gordon L. Lippitt, *Learning Theories and Training;* Training and Development Journal, April and May 1966. Reprint series, Leadership Resources, Inc., Washington, D. C.

Conference Arrangements

MARGARET MEAD
The American Museum of Natural History

    The conference situation is designed as one to permit the participants to act as whole individuals, using all their senses as they seldom do in the narrower, more specialized contexts of other forms of professional and academic life. The arrangements for the conference and the creation and management of the conference style are second only in importance to the facilitation of the substantive intellectual exchange.

    The expectations with which participants attend a conference play an important part in its success. Attempts are sometimes made to involve the participants in preconference activities, not only in the choice of other participants and in the preparation of materials, but in matters of choice of site, duration, program, etc. Any involvement of some of the participants—as participants, not as the initiating formal program committee—and not others is very hazardous. Differing patterns of expectation, often combining optimistic and gloomy forecasts, may grow up; subgroups may be formed by those who share the same fears, and preconference clusters may form who continue to oppose or subvert either the announced plans of the conference management or the developing plans of the conference group.[1]

---

[1] The consequences of the formation of such a dissenting group which is dissatisfied with the state of planning for a conference or for a larger meeting are likely to be cumulative. Thus, in 1948, when the Second World Congress on Mental Health was to be held to launch the new World Federation for Mental Health, one of the originators, the American psychiatrist, Dr. Harry Stack Sulli-

---

Reprinted by special permission from THE SMALL CONFERENCE by Margaret Mead and Paul Byers, Humanities Press, Inc., New York, New York.

It is better if all future participants have as uniform pre-conference expectations as possible. Pseudo-consultation should be particularly avoided, for example, requests for suggestions about conference procedures which have already been decided on. The initial invitation should contain as many items of information as possible—date, place, duration, and list of participants—but none of these arrangements should be circulated if they are likely to be changed. These items should either be stated as not yet decided upon, and the reasons given, or as decided upon and the reasons given. For example, the statement that a conference group is to be limited to 20 because of the size of the conference room in the conference site which has already been selected, or that only English speakers will be invited because facilities or funds are lacking for interpretation, is very much more satisfactory than such statements as that the group cannot be very much larger than 20 or that it will probably not be possible to arrange for interpretation. It is particularly important that every acceptance by a proposed participant be firm before the list of those expected is circulated. In almost all conferences that are planned far in advance

---

van, became concerned about the plans. He felt that there was danger that the element in the plan which provided for an international voluntary organization to support the work of the newly appointed director of the World Health Organization, Dr. Brock Chisholm, would be lost sight of in the kind of planning being done by the staff located in London. He therefore succeeded in getting a new group organized known as the International Preparatory Commission which would meet for two weeks before the large Congress, and prepare the ground for the Congress itself. The London staff, working under the leadership of Dr. Rees who had conceived and directed the worldwide preparations for the Congress, were excluded from much of this planning. None of them attended the two-week conference except for short periods and cocktail parties, but the International Preparatory Commission was expected to take into account the several hundred "pre-Congress" reports of small preparatory commissions that had been formed around the world. These reports had already been sent to London, and professional analysts had been employed to organize them into a number of sections. Speakers were chosen for each of the five days of the Congress, who were supposed to draw upon these partially summarized and organized reports in presenting one of the topics under which they were organized. These speakers were also participants in the preconference. When the preparatory commission, more interdisciplinary and international and ambitious in scope than any previous conference that had ever been convened met, the conference group faced these conflicting objectives. Dr. Sullivan was determined that the whole effort should be directed towards the support of Dr. Chisholm's policies. The Commission had a mandate to use the worldwide commission reports. The chairman of the Commission, Dr. L. K. Frank, who had not been involved in the London planning, saw it as a possibility to develop a coherent and organized, interdisciplinary and international statement on mental health (International Preparatory Commission, 1948). The participants had a variety of personal stakes and hidden agendas, as newcomers, as speakers at the Congress that was to follow, as political figures in

there will be one or two losses through illness, death, or changes in professional obligations. These are blows to the conference design and to the expectations of the participants. They also provide too-easy alibis for conference failures. In any case they should not be compounded by the circulation of lists of future participants which are unrealistic. Correspondingly, invitations should contain a firm clause about the date at which those who are invited must make up their minds whether to accept or decline.

In the conditions of today's world, conference dates have to be set either very far ahead, or with almost no warning at all. Each procedure has disadvantages. The conference set for a year ahead is subject to attrition of membership and sometimes of staff, and to unforeseeable conflicts of other sorts. Yet it does permit participants to plan ahead, to do relevant reading and thinking in advance, and to dovetail a particular conference with other travel considerations. Especially in conferences where participants are gathered from great distances, other considerations—simple desire to travel, a desire to visit a particular laboratory or library, the need to combine financed and unfinanced travel—will all enter in. These are inevitable and legitimate accompaniments of

---

the emerging field of mental health in their own countries, as persons committed to seeing that mental health did not become a substitute for religion or ideology or as persons committed to trying to accomplish this very aim. Early in the Commission meeting Dr. Sullivan, who had inaugurated it as, in a sense, a counter move to the plans of the principal organizers in London, tried to subvert his own creation by selecting a small group of kindred spirits and taking them away from the conference for a day and a night of private planning and revelry. The schism introduced into a conference already overloaded with conflicting objectives was never healed.

The fact that the International Preparatory Commission had been organized separately from the central planning presided over by Dr Rees meant that when the members of the International Planning Commission tried to perpetuate their planning role within the new organization, the World Federation for Mental Health, this role was never fully accepted. A long series of transformations which included an attempt to convert it into a panel of individuals, to reconstitute it as a standing advisory group, and finally to reconstitute it as a committee of the Executive Board all failed. These failures carried with them other schisms in the staff and among active and devoted members of the World Federation and were contributory to the period of disorganization of the Federation after the retirement of Dr. Rees in 1961.

Such complex repercussions need not be anticipated in the pure substantive conference which has no connection with larger administrative or organizational bodies. These hazards are indeed one reason why it is desirable not to use the complete conference style for the deliberations of commissions, standing committees, subsections, working parties, etc. The intensity of emotion generated by conference groups is tremendously facilitative of thought, but is also conducive to the formation of cliques, and schisms within larger bodies.

attendance at conferences at a distance but they also present hazards such as participants arriving late or leaving early because of unanticipated conflicts with other engagements. The further ahead the conference date is announced the more subsidiary plans of this sort the participants will make. Such subsidiary plans combined with inevitable disgruntlement and disappointment are compounded if the conference date lies far in the future and is also indefinite.

The conference that is convened suddenly with almost no warning has other drawbacks. It requires a really strong rationalization for the lack of warning, and if the poor planning that is almost inevitable is also justified by the same set of explanations used to justify the suddenness, a good deal of resentment is likely to be generated. A strenuous attempt to bring the planning up to standard—perhaps by a conscious attempt to avoid any innovations in conference style—is needed for these hastily convened meetings which participants are very likely to feel show a lack of respect for their individual responsibilities. Also, the frequent attempt to save money by placing a conference immediately before or after another meeting is likely to be seen as a fatiguing imposition especially if financial stringency has been invoked in the case of the original meeting. If the justification to be used is saving travel effort or travel time for participants who have to make long journeys, then the arrangements should reflect the actual desire to prevent fatigue instead of in fact calling for an additional amount of work which is seen as exploitation.[2]

---

[2] The recent conference on Urgent Anthropology convened by the Smithsonian Institution in Washington, D. C. over Easter, 1966, is a case in point. The planners justified the choice of the date on three different grounds. Many ethnologists from abroad would be in the United States for the annual presentation of the Wenner Gren Medal in Anthropology. This presentation had already been combined with a conference on nomadic peoples. The second justification was the sudden availability of some blocked funds that could be used for the transportation of more participants from overseas. The choice of Easter was further justified because most organizations respect Easter as a holiday, do not schedule conferences then, and so Easter was particularly suitable for assembling participants at short notice. The planning committee then added a totally new and only partly thought-out feature. It was announced that various administrative and elected federal officials in one way or another concerned with the subject of the conference had been invited for the last day of the conference. The exceedingly heterogeneous group of senior ethnologists from many countries were asked to prepare to give a sort of charade representing the deliberations of the preceding two days to these expected visitors. As could have been predicted, this combination of haste, expediency, lack of preparation and very great fatigue, with an unfamiliar, and because of the political implications, suspect innovation, produced an out-

Participants should also be given as clear a picture as possible of all the arrangements which are fixed in advance: the location, type of site, exact distance and kind of transportation needed from some large center, like London or Paris or Geneva; what the living conditions will be; what out-of-pocket expenses will be incurred; what free time, during the day, and the weekend, may be planned for; what arrangements there are for a participant to get away from the conference site; and the possibility of asking friends or colleagues to reach him by telephone, or to visit him during free periods. In order to give future participants such information, the conference staff have to have it, and they have to have decided just what responsibility for the program they must or can take in advance. Many of the avoidable difficulties that face conferences are due to lack of clarity and consistency on this very simple point. Conference planners announce plans and then do not carry them out or matters are referred to the group after they have been announced as settled. The ideal of flexibility is heavily abused as participants are first told that there will be no afternoon or no evening meetings, and then later it is suggested that "we set up our program as we go along."

If there is a clear framework, chairman and participants, technicians and interpreters, and conference center staff can work within it. Alternatively, every element must be left free, coffee breaks must be completely movable, interpreters asked to work at any hour and for any length of time, and participants warned in advance that it will be impossible for them to make any plans of any kind whatsoever.

The choice of conference site is extremely important, especially for the conference that is to meet only once and remain a unique event, and for the first conference in a unique series. For such conferences the site itself should have distinction and style and should provide the kind of setting that can be used to shape as rapidly as possible the developing conference ethos.

The unique conference also demands a setting in which the participants live and work together in as much isolation from all other groups or demands as possible. There are often proposals to hold conferences in large cities to save money or

---

burst of irrational protest and refusals of cooperation. Part of the potentially felicitous outcome of the entrepreneurial skill which had indeed seized upon a unique opportunity to advance an important cause was lost.

to take advantage of various kinds of facilities provided by the offices of the host organization, to save the cost of transporting staff and equipment, to use stationary interpretation equipment, etc. Although such considerations may seem to be a powerful argument in favor of locating a conference in a city with sleeping and eating quarters separated from the conference center, there is really very little to be said for them when weighed against the advantages of the unity and harmony that can be attained if a suitable isolated conference site such as those which have been established in the last 20 years in the United States, the United Kingdom, Europe and other parts of the world can be found.[3]

There are, however, choices to be made between luxurious and beautiful centers, such as Ditchley Park, and centers where austerity and frugality prevail. It seems clear that an extreme degree of luxury or frugality is better than conference sites which have neither the delights of luxury nor the moral rewards of frugality; either luxury or frugality may serve to make an occasion tolerable and memorable for those who share it together.

A first consideration should be the source of the funds. If the host organization belongs to a type of organization that is conceived of as affluent, luxury and beauty can be gracefully accepted as part of generous hospitality. This sense of generosity enhances the participants' pleasure in the conference and increases their willingness to discharge their part of the pact, to work hard, reread transcripts, send in additional information, and so on.

If, however, the conference is being paid for by an organization with limited finances to which the conference participants are also contributors, a quite different set of problems arises. In this case, participants may feel that all luxury is inappropriate and that the most severe austerity is called for. If, however, some of the participants are guests who have had no previous association with the struggling and impoverished organization, they may feel the economies and inconveniences imposed upon them express a failure of respect for them and their capacities. Whenever there is a marked attempt to find very frugal conditions, as in uncomfortable colleges or camps, it is important to weigh carefully how

---

[3] Examples are Arden House, outside New York, Ditchley Park and Roffey Park in England, the Villa Serballioni, Bellagio, Italy, Baguio in the Philippines, and the Benedictine Monastery at Bouake, Ivory Coast.

expensive the inconveniences are likely to be, and how much of a participant's energy is used up waiting for a single telephone or trying to find the way across an English college courtyard in the dark. Participants who will accept necessary discomforts as congruent with the capacities of certain kinds of organizations and certain kinds of conference aims, are very likely to chafe articulately against any inconveniences which seem to serve no useful purpose. The discovery in the middle of a conference that isn't going too well, that a much more comfortable spot could have been obtained, or was indeed actually offered, for the same, or even a lower cost, can significantly contribute to disaffection.

If a conference is a later one in a series, or part of long series where the members meet once a month, for example, like the University Seminars at Columbia, the criteria for a suitable site are very different. Rapid accessibility for a meeting lasting only a few hours, and a great familiarity with all the conditions, are a major requirement. And when there are many conferences held in connection with a single sponsoring organization like one of the United Nations agencies, the Macy Foundation, or the American Academy of Arts and Sciences, then the use of the same facilities is very desirable as the staff can become expert in managing them.

The actual technical facilities that exist or can be easily installed are a significant part of the conference site and no amount of charm, gardens, or scenery will make up for faulty electric conditions which prevent the tape recorder microphones and projectors from working. Duplicating equipment is often an essential part of conference procedure. The table and chairs themselves are important; hollow squares made of small tables are not a substitute for a solid table even if table coverings are introduced to hide participants' legs. One reason why all of these facilities are so important is that conference participants are people who give freely of their time. No one should ever be given an honorarium for attending a conference, although of course transportation, hospitality, and sometimes the expenses of or even remuneration for the preparation of papers or an editing job are appropriate. A conference must be a self-rewarding experience. In these circumstances participants have a right to feel that their contribution of time should be matched by adequate technical services.

However, in providing types of technical settings it is becoming apparent that a generation is growing up who, having been exposed to the best setting, are more able to function well in the worst. The setting which was once essential in order to convey some crucial aspect of conference style, such as the chairman ostentatiously taking off his jacket to indicate informality, ceases to be necessary as all the participants have attended conferences with informality built in. From then on, participants can take off their jackets or not.[4]

The way in which the conference is to be divided between formal sessions and informal periods between sessions, and the formality of the sessions themselves, both have to be taken into account in arranging the conference rooms. The more complicated the recording, the more important the conference room itself is and the more specialized its use has to be. A room that can give high visibility to all participants (which means a round not an oblong table) and that has or can be equipped with the other necessary accompaniments—light, visible blackboards or poster paper easels, projection equipment, interpretation equipment—then becomes a central requirement. And as such complex arrangements necessarily constrain participants to sit in the same seats and keep their chairs in approximately the same positions, the need for complementary informal arrangements for eating and talking together is increased. Dining facilities which permit small groups to form, pair conversations to occur, and

---

[4] At a recent conference in the United Kingdom, almost every rule of how to run a conference was violated; the organizer asked for advice from future participants which he did not intend to take; names of people who had refused to participate were circulated as future members of the conference; there was a requirement for a written paper which was to be handed to the editor just before the speaker, at a point stated on a fixed and rigid program, was to speak. The group sat in a circle with no table of any sort and the speaker was required to speak from a lectern placed at one side of the circle. The speaker was then encouraged to speak informally, rather than from his paper; when speakers then related what they said to the remarks of former speakers, the discussion of course referred to what the speaker said and not to the paper which he had written but did not read. The publication published the papers which had not been read and part of the discussion which only partially applied to these papers. Yet, so experienced were most of the group, and so skillful the editing, that in spite of the number of violations of good conference procedure, it was a good conference and a good publication. It was almost as if the participants had incorporated the good arrangements of previous conferences and worked within an imaginary set of conditions which did not obtain at this particular one. There is a danger that such increased familiarity by older and experienced conference participants may lure conference managers into a false security, unless provision is made for periodically feeding back information into conference planning on the vicissitudes of inexperienced groups.

people to breakfast alone if they wish, have to be considered together with the need to accommodate larger groups, and provide against single individuals being left out. It is also important to have arrangements that permit private conversation. One large over-lighted living room where everyone is in full view of everyone else all evening can nullify the success of the previous conference session.

Food arrangements also can contribute or detract from the whole conference. There should be choice allowed of foods that occur in a simple state, like fruit or nuts, to comfort the stranger who finds the local food difficult. At some conferences people become so absorbed in what they are talking about that they pay no attention to what they are eating and if very large helpings are served they may end up with an unidentifiable sense of repletion and satiety which they may mistakenly attribute to the intellectual fare instead of the meals. Some people also become abnormally hungry when they are living at such a high pitch and it is important to have stimulants and snacks available, particularly late at night.

Drinking can be a source of pleasure or trouble both at intranational and international conferences. Unless the group consists of total abstainers, the absence of alcoholic drinks is likely to be regarded as a severe deprivation. And a great deal of energy may go into smuggling drinks onto the premises or in furtive expeditions in search of a drink. It may be taken as a general rule that drinks should be available on the premises. Either participants should pay for all their drinks under conditions which discourage treating, or the host organization should make certain kinds of drinks, like beer or wine at meals, freely available at all times of day. If the host organization provides cocktails only, or only one large dinner where all drinks flow freely, the almost inevitable result is that the participants drink too much. If drinks can be ordered at any time, and the glut and famine psychology is removed, it has been found that participants will drink less.

Changed rhythms of drinking have to be controlled. Mild conviviality the first evening with the statement that no work will be done until tomorrow is one way of setting a style. Heavy drinking before dinner is ruinous to conferences that have evening sessions. A big dinner party or an expedition

to some distant spot which involves a lot of drinking may
actually wreck a conference. Conditions under which a small
group who are forming into a dissident clique can go away
and drink together are particularly to be avoided.

The need for rest and recreation are partly functions of the
way the conference is defined as an absolutely delightful
interchange or very hard although very rewarding work. If
the first definition is accepted, then the hours outside the
conference will be seen as occasions for doing still more
pleasant things: listening to music, visiting the site of an
ancient temple, attending a play. The participants will feel
the need for more and more experiences to feed their heightened sensibilities. If the emphasis is put upon the very exacting work that is being done, the demand will be for periods
of rest. The ideal conference setting provides for a variety of
outdoor activities, walking, swimming, skiing, tennis, table
tennis, suitable for various degrees of athletic enthusiasm.
If, in addition to the definition of the conference as serious
and exacting work, the participants feel that pleasure is in-
compatible with the seriousness and urgency of the conference task, then expeditions can be arranged that will be
congruent with this serious intent. The group may visit
slums, or a new kind of housing project, a terrible example
of a rundown mental hospital, or the latest experiment in
providing ideal care for unmarried mothers. Their dedication
to their task can be sharpened by the horrible examples and
their enthusiasm quickened by the utopian ones.

If no relevant contrapuntal activities are provided for,
various inappropriate and destructive things may happen,
as a few members of the group think up pranks, engage in
practical jokes, or emotions that could easily have been chan-
nelled into some cathartic and satisfying form—like watching a theatrical performance of great beauty—become diffuse
and produce a sense of malaise and dysphoria.

When a conference lasts less than a week, leisure activities
that are not shared by the whole group are disruptive and
wasteful. The reason an isolated site is sought is so that a
continuous unity of experience can be attained, and incur-
sions from any unshared excursions to the outer world are
to be avoided. This includes the necessity of a refusal to
include participants who can only come for part of the time,
however individually desirable they may be. It also requires

planning for recreative events that the whole conference can share. Very often the easiest sort of expedition to plan is something that will be new to all the participants, a boat ride on a river none of them have ever seen, or a kind of event right outside their experience, like a horse race if the group is an academic one. For recurrent conferences, some event of this kind may become an annual event contributing to the group's sense of itself as existing in history. Such shallow but ardently held traditions may also, however, make it harder to absorb the one or two new members whose addition is essential to keeping an ongoing group from becoming too ingrown.

For conferences that last more than a week some relief from the intense continuous interpersonal relationship is usually desirable. More interaction with the surrounding community can be encouraged; weekends can be set aside as occasions when the participants can leave the group for trips, visits, or to temporarily rejoin their families. The ideal condition would be if each participant individually left the conference for some activity of his own choosing, and returned refreshed so that all participants had had a comparable experience of separation from the group. Unfortunately this is usually impossible. Some participants will have no individual plans; arrangements will have to be made for them to do something together. There is always the risk that they will thereafter constitute either a cluster which is more tightly knit than the whole conference or a group who feel that they have been somehow deprived.

There are special provisions that make it easier for women, young people, and also the technical personnel. Occasions when anyone has to take responsibility for paying for anyone else, on an expedition for example, or a meal taken in an outside restaurant, should be carefully planned so that tickets can be bought in advance, and the embarrassment avoided that arises when a woman is dependent upon male gallantry and initiative. Care should also be taken not to ask any participant whose status is different from the majority to perform extra menial tasks. Women participants should not be asked to make the tea, unless pouring tea is seen as a special privilege. Young people may be brought in specifically to do certain kinds of work; this is sometimes a way of including them. But then they should not be asked to do additional chores because they are young. If various types of technical specialists, interpreters, or conference secretaries, are included socially in the group then their full social status should not be called in question by sudden capricious requests to do chores.

The question of what to do with wives—or very occasionally husbands—who are not concerned with the subject of the conference is recurrently difficult. If the conference also contains professional women without accompanying husbands, the presence of wives may produce uncomfortable dichotomies, as the wives come to be seen as appropriate companions for relaxation while the professional women are designated as partners of the working hours. Each group may resent this compartmentalization. If accompanying wives are bored, they may set up negative extrasession resonances. The device of giving men a choice as to whether or not they wish their wives to accompany them may work well for a single conference. The wives who enjoy conferences will be brought and most of those who do not will be left at home. But if the conference is one of a series, very few wives will tolerate glowing reports on a conference that they might have but did not share without demanding to accompany their husbands to the next one. On the whole, the exclusion of all nonparticipants and the admission, without prejudice, of professional participants who happen to stand in the relationship of husband and wife, brother and sister, or parent and child, seems to be the safest course. Some evening gaiety contributes to a conference if the planners remember that women have to have time to dress for many occasions for which men can wear their daytime clothes.

All occasions when the level of amusement is lowered from that which is customary for this type of group, excessive drinking, the presence of women of lower social status, visits to dives, gambling, etc., are to be avoided. If a few participants insist on such activities it is better to break the rule of total group attendance. Conferences with more men than women are easier to manage than conferences with more women than men. Care should be taken not to provide living arrangements where two or three women participants are isolated in some way from the rest of the group, or in any way to insist that the small number of women must associate with each other more than they associate with the male members of the conference.

A conference group has a life of its own and like all living things needs to be cherished. An important part of conference management, is a lively awareness of what is happening in the group. Is any member showing signs of illness or too great strain? Is the pace of the group slackening unaccountably? If there are unexpected signs of strain are they to be referred to something happening within the group—a festering misunderstanding for example.[5]

A style of dealing with difficulties of this sort has been developed within the group dynamics field in which a group dynamics specialist would bring the difficulties into the consciousness of the group. While this is an efficient way of training group discussion leaders and group therapists, it is destructive and inefficient in dealing with a group of intellectuals who have met to use their minds, in concert, and who may already be finding the conference experience unfamiliar and possibly painful. To add to the burdens they are carrying any sort of public group self-analysis is most inadvisable.

The more desirable course is for someone, either the chairman or the appropriate staff member, to try to diagnose the source of the difficulties and make plans for shifting the mood, giving individuals information that they obviously lack, getting someone who is ill and whose illness is being reflected in the group to bed or to a doctor. Whether the actual precipitating difficulty is external or internal to the conference, it should be dealt with as external to the main

---

[5] In a recent conference composed of anthropologists and a few biologists, one of the anthropologists expressed the hope that the anthropologists, who were in the overwhelming majority, would be careful not to get involved in any *intra*disciplinary discussions. One of the biologists, whose readiness to mishear was probably a function of the discrepant numbers, heard this statement as an admonition to have no *inter*disciplinary discussion. As the conference had been called as an interdisciplinary one, this was obvious nonsense, but his belief, and his resultant resentment, was sufficiently contagious so as to go a long way towards spoiling a conference already heavily rationed in the time allotted to an important topic.

At another conference at which there were an unusually large number of psychoanalysts, the conference group contained the former analyst of the chairman and this unexpected circumstance complicated or precipitated a near-psychotic episode in the chairman.

Participants who are untrained in disciplining their intuitions may pick up unconscious strains between members and harp on them mischievously and destructively.

purposes of the conference itself. The conference period is all too short, the communication of the content far too valuable to use it as an occasion for any sort of moral or psychological therapy.

The announced presence of a group dynamics specialist, either as an observer or a group therapist, is likely to be highly resented also because his presence violates the requirement of total commitment to the principal purpose of the conference. Instead conference management skills should involve sensitivity to group process and a willingness to incorporate this sensitivity within the participant role.

But there is another sense in which the conference group needs protection. They need to be sustained through the frustration and near despair that is a predictable part of any conference. From one point of view, this participant despair would seem comparable to the postpartum depression of a woman after the birth of her first child. It is an unfamiliar experience from which she has to be rescued by the counsel of a trusted older woman who can assure her that all recently parturient women feel like this and she will get her strength back soon. But there is a difference. The pessimism and despair that sets in about a quarter of the way through a conference is also functional. Those who feel it most acutely will then make an extra effort to surmount whatever difficulties in communication have developed. Too much reassurance by the overexperienced may in such cases do harm.[6]

But provision must be made to provide conditions under which an extra effort can be made, or some time found for an extra recess during which individuals can consult and stimulate each other.

The duration of the conference will impose a rhythm and the intensity of the interchange a style. Sometimes a conference experience is given enormously heightened intensity through the dissolution of barriers due to hierarchy or formal professional rivalry, race or class prejudice, or simple cross-disciplinary ignorance. When this happens, something akin to a conversion may occur. For other participants, the expe-

---

[6] At the Eastborne conference on conferences the highly experienced group of participants predicted when the slump would occur but failed to take this functional aspect into account. Instead, most of them went out for the free evening. If two of the members had not realized that failure to do anything about the recognized slump was in fact really dangerous, the conference might in fact have been a failure.

rience may have some of the quality of heightened perception that comes from falling in love. Those with eidetic
imagery may fall asleep with the faces of every member
etched on their eyeballs or the voices of each ringing in
their ears. For others the emergence of a new conceptualization may be primarily an aesthetic experience.

It is useful to provide for the need for some kind of ritual
to end a period of such intensity. One device is to plan for
some appropriate ritual beginning—such as each member
speaking briefly about his hopes, or his reason for being
there—which can be paralleled by a closing ritual in which
each member speaks again. Such repetitions in effect set the
conference experience off from the rest of life and free the
participants to leave the conference scene. If the conference
is one of a series, however, it may be more desirable to have
no closing ceremony whatsoever, and leave the unresolved
feelings to carry over to the next year and the next. In such
cases it may even be better to let the conference trail off
with people leaving at different times and without farewells.
But for the single conference there should be closure. Lists
of the addresses of each participant should be distributed.
Clear plans for publication or records should be announced.
The closing time should have been realistically set in relation to transportation and participants should be told that
they are expected to stay to the end. A closing meal to which
everyone need not stay may then provide just the necessary
flexibility.

Finally a perennial problem is whether observers are to be
allowed. This takes different forms, as demands come in to
let other members of the institution where the conference is
being held, a university, a government agency, an institute,
have some part in what is going on. And in some instances
a conference may be held as a way of strengthening a program, establishing better relationships within an institution
or in a whole community. If the conference is held on the
campus, at the hospital, inside the agency building, these
requests to include observers are exceedingly difficult to re-
fuse. All of these problems are summarily solved if the conference is held in some isolated spot far from other institutions and community pressures. Then some single event, or
in the case of a long conference, several events—a cocktail
party, a reception, a lecture or series of lectures given by the

conference members in other settings—are ways of maintaining good relations and still refusing to admit observers.

But where the physical circumstances and the social pressures makes the refusal of admission to all observers impossible, the problem can be solved in several ways. A room in which the conference group sit round a table while the observers sit further back and preferably on raised seats as in an operating theatre, can be combined with a large visible clock, synchronized with the recording equipment. Observers may be requested to write comments or questions, with the time exactly noted, and these can be taken into account in future sessions, or by the editor if some report is projected. This method has the advantage of giving the observers a sense of participation yet keeping the actual inter-acting conference group small, and reducing resentment on the part of the observers and guilt on the part of the conference members.

Another arrangement which, however, requires a more complicated physical setting, is to have the proceedings of the conference broadcast or televised to another room. Although superficially television would appear to be the more satisfactory technique, there are certain objections as the process of watching television seems to draw people into themselves and away from each other like the act of looking intently through a keyhole. For the individual observer seated alone, or at least in complete independence of the other observers, a small television set is eminently satisfactory and provides the advantage of a close-up of the participants' faces. But if there are a group of observers—students, members of other departments, foreign visitors—who are in any way related to each other in the sense that they may later discuss the proceedings or take part in some social occasions with the conference participants, television viewing may serve to isolate them from each other. Broadcasting on the other hand draws the group of listeners closer together, as if the voice that appears to be actively addressing each, were in fact addressing all.

Whichever of these two methods is used, the participants should be aware that the observers are there and should have a chance to inspect the room in which the observers will gather.

If only sound is used, the observers should have some opportunity to see the participants. Television is sometimes used to protect the sensibilities of some member of the group as, for example, when a psychiatric case conference at which the patient is present is televised to a distant larger group of medical students. Such procedures should not be confused with televising a conference. Televising or broadcasting a conference to observers is analogous to the use of one-way screens to observe children at play, or of telescopic lenses to observe deer on the range; the presence of the observer on the spot would disturb the proceedings although there is nothing secret or confidential about them. Even a single observer destroys the ideal atmosphere of total involvement which every good conference needs.

SECTION II

CONFERENCE

TECHNOLOGY

Improving Large Group Meetings

LELAND P. BRADFORD and STEPHEN M. COREY

Because the large group meeting is a venerable social institution, we seldom investigate and try to meet the basic needs and problems of the people who attend the large group meeting, or experiment with various methods of planning and conducting meetings so as to improve their effectiveness, or make much effort to study the effectiveness of such a meeting after it is over. The literature critically examining meetings attended by a large number of people is practically nonexistent. What experimentation has been conducted is typically directed toward the improvement of the platform presentations.

In a previous article [1] one of the authors analyzed some of the basic patterns of action typical of most large group meetings. The present paper has been written primarily to call attention to the importance of audience dynamics in contrast to looking only at what happens on the platform. In order to do this, we first indicate the necessary integration between large group meetings and other rather typical conference activities, such as small discussion groups, subcommittee meetings, and other kinds of working groups. As conferences have developed in recent years from the convention type of speaker-dominated program to the work con-

Reprinted by special permission of ADULT EDUCATION BULLETIN, of the Department of Adult Education of the National Education Association of the United States, and of the authors.

[1] Bradford, Leland P. "Leading the Large Meeting." *Adult Education Bulletin* 14: 38-50; December 1949.

ference, increasing attention has been given to planning the
conference general sessions so that they contribute to the
total purpose of the conference. This is not easy to do.

Second, we describe examples of actual meetings in order
to illustrate various techniques designed to meet the many
audience needs usually overlooked and to show how the
large meeting can be used in an intensive and complicated
training program in human relations skills. Training in these
skills is receiving increasing attention by many groups.

The Weaknesses in Most Large Group Meetings

In the article referred to above, some basic weaknesses
of the conventional large group meeting were commented
upon: (a) the phenomenon of audience passivity induced by
listening only; (b) the anonymity phenomenon of being
lost in a mass instead of belonging to a working group;
(c) the rejection phenomenon of resisting suggested changes
made from the platform because the speaker is different from
the audience member and does not understand his problems;
and (d) the "one-way communication" phenomenon, which
prevents the interchange of point of view and information at
problem points that is essential for real communication.

We do not mean to imply that the conventional type of
large group meeting cannot be effective or that skill in speaking and the possession of sensitivity to audience emotional
reactions are not important. The point we would like to make
is that the large group meeting is apt to be successful to
the degree that its purposes are consistent with the varying
and complex needs of the audience and to the degree that
it has been planned and conducted in such a way as to
achieve these purposes.

The planning of most large group meetings rests, unfortunately, upon some questionable assumptions. One is
that the small group "responsible" for the meeting, or the
speakers themselves, should make the decisions regarding
the problems to be dealt with. A second belief that often gets
in our way is that "telling" a large group, or the momentary
uplift and covert mental promises made to themselves by
the audience members, is sufficient to bring about change.
We often assume, too, that the best way to improve the
large group meeting is to pay more attention to platform
oratory, to improved media of communication such as films,

or to other mechanical devices such as public-address systems. Tradition, the undoubted effectiveness of some conventional large group meetings, the appeal made to all of us by the expert speaker, and fear of what may happen if control of the meeting leaves the platform have conspired to make these assumptions persist.

Problems of the Large Group Meeting

Any attempt to examine large group meetings in respect both to audience and platform behavior indicates not only the complexity of the forces that are operating but also the great potentials for learning, for social action, and for social change that do exist when large groups get together to achieve a common purpose. Traditionally, we view the success of the large meeting as being dependent primarily upon forces emanating from the platform. In reality, many additional forces also contribute to the reaction of audience members, such as the expectations of members of the audience, their reasons for coming to the meeting, and their desire for active participation. Any examination of the large-group meeting phenomena indicates the following as some of the areas to which attention must be given:

1. *The purpose of the meeting.* While most large meetings do have an educational purpose, they illustrate an exceedingly wide range of specific purposes—to give information, to inspire, to entertain, to bring about group decision making or problem solving, to induce change in the individual audience member, or to bring the audience as a group to engage in activity leading toward a specific social change. Each of these purposes may require a different type of meeting, and the importance of being clear about the purpose of the large meeting in relation to the audience needs and the methods employed cannot be overemphasized.

2. *Platform-audience intercommunication.* Effective communication is always a two-way process. In order for communication to be maximally effective, definite arrangements must be made to insure the active involvement of all members of the group whether or not this involvement is verbally overt. This active involvement and participation on the part of people in the audience, as well as people on the platform, is a complex psychosociological phenomenon.

3. *Understanding audience behavior.* Members of the audience are reacting to many events. They are affected not only by what happens on the platform but also by the presence of other people in the audience. Too, the members of the group are variously motivated. The total psychosociological atmosphere of the audience-platform situation may be such as to establish decided resistances to the communication of platform presentation, or it may, on the other hand, facilitate understanding and acceptance. Some members of the audience may be seeking an opportunity to be heard by others, to contribute actively to the meeting. Other members of the group may wish to remain hidden and passive. Despite these differences among individuals, there are general patterns of audience needs—the need to participate in the meeting, the need to be accepted by others, the need for reinforcement through discovering that others face the same problems and have the same reactions—that should be met in order to increase the success of the meeting.

4. *Platform-audience collaboration.* Successful meetings are most likely to be those in which there is a real feeling that the gap between the platform and the audience has been closed and that both groups are engaged in a common task. While it is true that exceedingly effective public speakers frequently are able to create the illusion that there is no gap, in the typical large meeting a substantial space exists between the audience and the platform.

5. *The place of the meeting in a wider setting.* Too frequently, large meetings are planned as if they had or could have no relationship to events that take place before and after the meeting. We believe that if the purpose of the meeting is other than pure entertainment, it must take its place as part of a larger plan. If this is not done—if the meeting is not designed so as to be derived from and move on to another experience or activity or change—then it tends to be a psychologically self-contained unit bringing about its own closure, which tends to preclude change.

These are only some of the areas that should be studied if large group meetings are to be made more effective. As those persons responsible for planning and conducting such meetings are able to reach a better understanding of basic audience needs, they will come increasingly to recognize that their work involves more than securing a speaker or a film and advertising the meeting. Arranging for and conducting large group sessions are complex tasks. One serious problem is the strong personal need of many speakers to be allowed to speak uninterruptedly to others. While information or inspiration provided by a speaker is occasionally called for, the role of resource person to the audience has almost unlimited possibilities that are as yet relatively unexplored.

General Sessions at an NTL Institute Laboratory

The case examples described below are selected from a larger number of general meetings held at one of the summer sessions of the NTL Institute for Applied Behavioral Science[2] which involved about 150 persons. Because the laboratory was concerned with training for work with groups, each general session had at least a dual purpose. One involved trying to meet a somewhat specific training need, such as reaching a better understanding of group-member roles. A second purpose was to provide all who attended the laboratory with an opportunity to participate in and experiment with methods of conducting large meetings. Consequently, efforts were made to use a wide variety of techniques. We had planned to conduct research on the effectiveness of these large group methods, but unanticipated scheduling and personnel problems precluded carrying these plans through. All participants, however, did fill in postmeeting reaction sheets after most of the general sessions. These reactions enabled the participants to indicate the extent to which they liked or disliked the meeting and to state the reasons for their judgments. These postmeeting reactions were used by the general-sessions committee to improve subsequent meetings, and, whenever possible, they were condensed and reported back to the participants.

The general sessions described below were selected to illustrate both the range of meeting purposes at the labora-

---

[2] A specific laboratory at one of the NTL Institute's past summer programs has been selected for illustrative purposes. While this particular laboratory has its own unique design features plus some historical aspects, many of the techniques and design elements have been employed since by various staff members in many other laboratories.

tory and the methods employed in conducting the meetings. In addition to information and training goals, these meetings attempted to meet basic group needs by fulfilling the following functions:

1. Provide opportunity for audience members to become actively involved in the meeting
2. Provide audience members with opportunities to express themselves to the audience
3. Improve clarity of understanding of the problems or topics under consideration
4. Enable all members of the laboratory to collaborate in problem solving, rather than having the solution come from the platform
5. Provide reinforcement to the audience member through realization that his problem is one that others face as well
6. Make it possible for each audience member to identify actively with the problem.

A number of different methods and techniques in various combinations—buzz sessions, sensitizing panels, panel discussions, small-group exchange of questions and answers, listening teams, role playing, interview reporting, mimeographed directions for audience participation—were used to achieve these purposes.

The seven large meetings described illustrate the three sequential stages of laboratory need—for orientation, for participation in training, for planning for back-home use.

First General Orientation Session

Participants in any conference, training program, or series of meetings come with many different expectations, purposes, and needs. Usually a considerable time elapses before these become identified and integrated, if they ever do, into a common purpose and plan of working that meets most of the needs of the individuals. Productivity could be measurably increased if such conferences could start in high rather than in low gear. Typically, conference planners hope to start in high gear by providing an emotional uplift through a fine speech. Such uplift is only of momentary value unless the speech meets the basic need of the participant to find a place in the conference that is within his ability, enables him to recognize his contributions, and leads toward the solution of the problems which caused his attendance. This rarely results from an address.

In planning for this first important orientation session of the laboratory, the following problems were recognized by the staff:

1. The participants' need to get acquainted and to feel at home
2. The importance of getting out into the open and seeing the validity of the many different purposes for coming to the conference as well as the expectations regarding what will happen. Otherwise these differences in purpose and expectation will remain as hidden agenda items for each individual, blocking and distorting his participation
3. Communication ambiguity resulting from differences in vocabulary among different groups of participants and between staff and participants
4. The effect of status upon interpersonal relations
5. The participants' need to get a clear picture of the total laboratory plan, so that the various parts would take on proper meaning
6. The participants' need to know the various staff members responsible for such services as housing and the administrative structure, so they would know whom to approach on various problems
7. The participants' need to gain immediate understanding of the pattern of behavior at the laboratory, the degree of informality, and so on
8. The participants' need to become involved as soon as possible in the process of orientation. Orientation should not be done to them, but by them.

The first general orientation session of the laboratory was held on the evening of the day during which all the participants arrived in Bethel. This meeting was planned by a special conference committee as part of a total orientation program that involved meeting the participants, accompanying them to their living quarters, and providing them with maps and other general materials, a picnic supper, and a series of "progressive parties" at the homes of staff members. These over-all orientation plans were considered and criticized by the entire staff group during the week of training preceding the conference.

The general orientation session consisted of several major activities. First, there was a brief statement of welcome and introduction of a few people from whom the participants might need specific services. This was followed by a role-playing situation acted out by participants and chaired by one of the conference staff members. This role playing was relatively spontaneous, but those who participated had been identified previously and had planned the types of roles they would play. The role players had spent most of the afternoon interviewing as many participants as possible in order to communicate to the total general-session group some of the expectations and possible anxieties that existed within the participant body. The role-playing scene, consisting of a group interview, helped give the data collected by participants from other participants concerning their worries and expectations a human quality that would not have been true if the facts had merely been presented by one person in a statistical summary.

Following this role playing, the participants were divided into a number of small buzz groups [3] to identify and to discuss further the problems and questions of an orientation nature that they would like the members of the laboratory staff to discuss or answer. One person from each of the buzz groups then reported the questions and problems raised. These were written on newsprint so that the total group might see them. Those that were sufficiently specific and concrete to be answered briefly were dealt with immediately by a panel of four staff members.

After the buzz session reports, one of the staff members made a quick analysis of audience feelings. He tried to develop a spirit of willingness to bring out problems and disagreements by attempting to indicate what audience members might hesitate to say and to crystallize the efforts of those participating in this orientation session to meet the many problems of participants and the results of these efforts.

Finally, participants were given a brief overview of the kinds of activities they might expect during the three weeks they would be working together.

One of the major problems facing any conference or training institute is that of insuring that desirable change take place in the activities of the participant after he returns home. The laboratory has tried, not always too successfully, to meet this problem by periodic consultations between various staff members and individual participants or teams,

---

[3] See page 29.

leading toward definite planning for ways in which learning at the laboratory can be applied elsewhere.

Session on Planning for Consultation on Back-Home Problems

The problems of consultation are multitudinous. How can it be made collaborative rather than having the participant come for an "answer"? How can the consultant strengthen himself against the beguilement that leads him to pretend omniscience? How can reasonable expectations about what can be done be established? How can the consultee think through his problem carefully enough before approaching the consultant so that the wisest possible use is made of the consultant? These and many others are questions that must be answered before adequate consultation on back-home problems can result.

This general session—held during the first week so that its results would affect consultation during the later periods of the laboratory—tried to open up the problem of collaboration between staff and participants on planning back-home use of laboratory learnings.

Seats were arranged on three sides of a cleared space. On one side were seated those participants who came as "teams." Another of the three sides was occupied by those who came as single members from a given organization or area. The third side included staff members, many of whom would be called upon to serve as consultants following the laboratory.

The meeting opened with a brief discussion of the problems of consultation, with a description of the method of the meeting in which all would be prepared to participate actively, and with an indication that the meeting would provide no answers, but would merely open up problems. Following this, a group of staff members put on a spontaneous dramatization in which a two-member team from an imaginary organization approached a member of the laboratory staff for help in planning on back-home problems. As the role-playing situation developed, it became clear to the audience that the team faced many problems beyond those it had planned to discuss with the consultant. One of the team members played the role of an extremely dominant woman who hardly allowed the other team member, a man, to speak to the consultant. The needs for attention and dominance upon the part of one team member illustrated some of the problems the team had in gaining acceptance in its own community. Again, the team had not thought through whether they were the ones in the community to tackle the particiular problem they were engaged in, the extent to which they should involve other people in the plan, or the extent to which there had been any realization on their part of the consequences of their activities in terms of final goals.

After the scene was played for a short time, the three sections of the audience broke into small buzz sessions to discuss the situation in respect to the inadequacies of preparation of the team, the type of consultation carried on by the consultant and its effects upon the team, the number of problems the consultant-consultee team did not recognize themselves, and things that might have been done by the consultant or by the consultee team in preparing for this situation.

Reports from the various buzz sessions were listed on the blackboard. After this, a real team was asked to plan for meeting with a staff member in front of the entire audience. The team was requested to take into consideration the previous role-playing scene as it may have affected their own team pattern. Three members of the staff sat behind this team and from time to time made comments to the audience which helped the group to see more deeply into the adequacy of the team planning. One of these staff members was a psychiatrist; another, a sociologist; and the third, a psychologist. Each commented from the point of view of his own professional background.

The session ended with a brief description of the laboratory machinery for planning interviews with those staff members or participants best suited to be of help in specific situations.

Session in Which a Representative Council Meets with its Constituents

All too frequently, in any organization or section of society, a gap gradually widens between a representative committee and the larger constituency that selected it. Only in a crisis does the constituency register reactions to the activities of its respresentatives.

The laboratory, during the first week, placed considerable emphasis upon the well-planned selection of six participants to join with five staff members on a steering committee which would make major decisions concerning the ongoing life of the laboratory in all its aspects—from problems of housing to decisions on change in training design. Because representation of participants was taken seriously, one general session was planned to help them reach a better understanding of the functioning of their own steering committee. This, furthermore, would illustrate problems of selecting and working with a representative committee and would give participants an opportunity to observe the effectiveness of their own representatives and thus check the adequacy of their process of selection.

This meeting was announced as an effort to improve communication between the steering committee and the remainder of the NTL Institute community. Because the committee, at the time, was faced with the necessity of reaching decisions on certain matters that concerned the participants, a good opportunity was at hand to involve all the participants in these decisions as well as to demonstrate the feasibility of co-operative thinking by a central committee and the constituent group it represented.

The meeting began with the steering committee on the platform as its chairman reviewed some of the problems on which the committee would have to make decisions. At several points, research information appropriate to the decision areas was presented to the steering committee and, of course, to the participants. This was not a rehearsed meeting. It was a regular steering committee session designed to identify some of the issues with which it had been dealing, to get a first look at some of the evidence that bore on these issues, and to make necessary decisions affecting the entire laboratory.

After this problem and data introduction, the participants were broken into discussion groups, with representatives to the steering committee meeting with their own constituent groups. Thus the steering committee could secure reactions of its constituents as well as their recommendations regarding actions that should be taken.

The meeting concluded with a reconvened meeting of the steering committee, during which reports were made of the consensus or near-consensus of feeling or judgment of the constituents. The steering committee then proceeded to take action on a number of problems.

Session Providing Audience Collaboration with a Speaker

One of the most common types of large group meetings includes an address by a well-known speaker. The sequence of events ordinarily goes like this: the visiting speaker is introduced fulsomely; he is listened to for an hour; the members of the group and the speaker reach some subjective judgment as to whether they like one another; both the audience and the speaker go home.

These consequences seem to result from the use of a speaker in this fashion:

1. The audience subjectively accepts or rejects the speaker.
2. There is passive and relatively generalized listening and, infrequently, a specific framework to enable audience members to listen critically.
3. The speaker gets no help or learning from the audience. He delivers, but does not receive.
4. There is no chance for the audience members to clarify certain points or expand others.
5. There is no opportunity for active collaboration between speaker and audience—no real working together on a common problem.

One of the laboratory general sessions attempted to develop collaboration between the audience and a well-known speaker so that each would be helped by the other. The speaker in this case was Stuart Chase, and the meeting was planned by a committee that included him. Specifically, the meeting purposes were to enable the participants to exchange their views about the speech before leaving the meeting place; to enable the speaker to hear and react to the reports of the discussions among the audience; to give the speaker help on his problems; and to demonstrate a different type of program built around the contributions of a main speaker.

In order to achieve these purposes, a program was planned which represented this sequence of events: (a) a general orientation statement explaining the purpose of the meeting to the audience, (b) distribution of a mimeographed sheet describing the procedures to be used (reproduced below), (c) introduction of the speaker, (d) the address, (e) formation of small discussion groups with specific directions, and (f) reports from each of these discussion groups with comments by the speaker.

These small discussion groups were, in effect, listening teams. Each was directed to attend particularly closely to some element or aspect of the address or some specific kind of help which the speaker wanted from the audience. The total general-session group was divided into halves. One half of the audience was especially responsible for identifying additional help that the laboratory group wanted from Mr. Chase. The other half of the audience had special responsibility for providing specific kinds of help to the speaker himself.

Each of these halves was further broken into small discussion groups and given the specific mimeographed directions reproduced on the next page.

The postmeeting reactions indicated that this general session was one of the most successful ones held.

Session on Concepts of Leadership

Frequently, in many conferences, interest in a specific problem or question builds up steadily to a point of considerable pressure and tension that can be reduced only through a thorough exploration of the problem. Because the laboratory put much of its training emphasis upon developing skills and sensitivities of group leadership, inevitably much interest and many differences of opinion among both participants and staff centered around questions of the ethics of leadership and the boundaries of leadership action in a democratic society.

Consequently, a general session was planned by a special committee which included participants and training leaders. Meeting purposes included not only a desire to arrive at conclusions but also the importance of indicating the complexity of the problem area.

Audience members were asked to sit with their training groups. There were also two groups of staff members who were not regular members of training groups. The program for the evening was divided into three major parts. Two separate discussions were to be held by the eight groups. Finally a small panel would react to the results of the discussions. As each audience member entered the hall, he was handed the directions reproduced on page 00.

As indicated, each group was directed to identify the two or three most important questions that had to do with leadership and membership roles and to which answers were wanted. These questions then were exchanged with another discussion group which spent its time during the last half of the period trying to formulate, to the best of its ability, what the answers to these questions might be. What this meant was that each discussion group formulated questions and then attempted to answer the questions that were formulated by another group.

At the end of this double discussion period, a representative from each of the discussion groups reported to the total population not only the questions that were raised by another group but also his group's answers to these questions.

The program was concluded by a panel of three members of the staff who discussed additional questions about leadership that were raised by people speaking from the floor.

Session Devoted to Reporting Research Findings

During the last week of the laboratory there was major emphasis upon analyzing results of research and training activities and planning for use in back-home situations. A pledge of the laboratory staff each year has been that all research data collected during the laboratory period that can possibly be analyzed in time will be reported back to the entire laboratory, even though the presentation is tentative. Such a presentation in a general session is difficult, because usually it means communicating rather technical information to persons of limited technical background. This problem is faced, in different variations, at many meetings.

For the general session reporting research findings, attempts were made to devise ways of improving communication. The session itself consisted largely of oral reports supported by visual aids and made by members of the various research teams. It would have been ideal to be able to do a practice run of the program before a panel of participants in order to check on and improve communication. Because time pressures precluded this, however, the planning committee employed a technique which would seem to have somewhat general applicability. The technique involved the use of a sensitizing panel. A number of the participants were asked to serve on this panel and were asked to interrupt and question the speakers whenever a member of the panel felt it necessary in order to clarify or define technical terms or consider practical implications. The members of this panel were chosen not only because of their similarity in background to most of the participants but also because of their willingness to speak out and make their uncertainties clear. They were also sensitive to the importance and types of findings to be reported and the desirability of all participants' understanding the meaning of the results.

Final Evaluation Session

Some kind of final evaluation session at the end of a conference or workshop is common. Ordinarily, the technique used involves informal expressions of an evaluative sort made orally before the total conference group plus reactions to some more formal questionnaire or opinionnaire. These reactions are later summarized by a staff in order to make better plans for the next conference.

The evaluation general session of the laboratory was somewhat different. The consensus of the special planning committee was that the "evaluations" should be heard and reacted to by all the participants. There was the further conviction that the participants should have an opportunity to engage in discussions about specific aspects of NTL which seemed crucial to them. Consequently, an evaluation session was arranged which involved these steps:

1. The committee, in consultation with participants, identified some 15 major questions regarding the laboratory that it felt should be considered in the evaluation. There was emphasis in these questions on the back-home behavior that might be a consequence of the conference.
2. These questions were numbered and mimeographed, and the entire laboratory group of staff and participants was broken into 15 discussion groups that met for about 40 minutes. A spokesman-recorder was named for each group.
3. Following the discussions, the spokesmen-recorders met in five subgroups to pool their findings.
4. The entire laboratory assembled in general session. A panel of five persons representing the five subgroups reported on the results of the 15 discussions. Comments were invited from the audience.

This plan was an effort to use discussion groups of longer duration and more formal structure than buzz sessions, to collect and systematize the thinking of a large number of people for presentation to the entire group. The entire program comprised no more than two hours.

The seven large meetings described in this article have been illustrations of attempts to meet, in a variety of ways, basic needs of audience members as well as to improve collaboration and communication between platform and audience. These meetings have not been described with any belief that they present tried-and-true methods of leading large meetings. Rather they picture an experimental approach to a complex problem.

Group Self-Analysis of Productivity in the Work Conference

RONALD LIPPITT

In the work conference, productivity depends not on the intelligence or eloquence of the guest speakers or on the creativity of the papers read by the participants, but rather on the adequacy with which the participants, working in small groups, define, break down, and solve certain problems they have selected.

In our better educational systems today, it is recognized that straight thinking and problem solving are a complex of individual skills that can be taught. We have discovered in our researches in group psychology that sharing in group problem solving requires a variety of group membership skills beyond those of individual problem solving. Time and again, we find a group of intelligent, individual problem solvers functioning together as a very unintelligent group who fail to set their goals adequately, pay little attention to the strategic organization of themselves in relation to the structure of the task, get all mixed up in interpersonal communication problems, fail to mobilize the group's intellectual resources, and resemble a neurotic patient in their incompetency in decision making. We have discovered, however, that most are eager and able to increase their competency if the opportunity to look analytically at their problems of group operation is present.

Reprinted by special permission of ADULT EDUCATION BULLETIN, of the Department of Adult Education of the National Education Association and of the author.

81

Because of this eagerness and ability of groups to do something about improving their own group productivity if the opportunity is provided, the technique of the group-productivity observer has been developed and used in a variety of work conferences, committees, and staff groups. The idea is a very simple one, although in most cases it results in profound effects upon group productivity far in excess of the energy and effort expended. There are four aspects to the process, which can be summarized as follows:

1. The group accepts the idea that no matter what their working responsibility is, it will be worthwhile to spend some effort on analyzing and improving their own procedures of working together.
2. Some person in the group takes the responsibility for functioning as an observer of group process. This is a special responsibility to the group just as is that of discussion leader, recording secretary, and the like.
3. Every member of the group is asked to check a brief post-meeting reaction or suggestion sheet at the end of each session, giving his own feelings about the meeting and about ways in which it might be improved.
4. Periodically, brief group evaluation sessions are held at which the observer reports the essence of his observations and advances certain hunches about improving group productivity from his observations and from the analysis of the meeting-reaction slips. These ideas are discussed and further interpretation and conclusions reached in group discussion.

Now take a look at what is involved in these four steps, as they are discussed below.

Group Understanding and Acceptance of Analysis of Its Own Productivity

First of all, the participants must have accepted the idea that they are coming to a genuine work conference where they will be working on problems of their own choosing as well as coming to a conference which they feel needs to be held. Second, it is desirable that each participant should receive before he comes to the conference a brief, clear statement of what is involved in the idea of a work conference, what is expected of him in terms of responsibility for group participation, and how he can expect the group leader, observer, and recorder to help the group. Third, the orientation session of the conference frequently presents a spontaneous demonstration on the stage of a work group in action, with an interpreter or clarifier pointing out to the audience various aspects of effective and ineffective group procedure.[1] During this demonstration the observer is pointed out and has an opportunity toward the end of the demonstration to function in leading a brief evaluation session. His role as a servant of the group rather than an "outside judge" is made clear.

The Observer and the Role of the Observer

We must keep three things in mind about the group-productivity observer: (a) He must be sensitive and objective in noting aspects of group operation which can be improved. (b) He must be a person who is accepted freely and easily by the group. (c) He must be able to verbalize his observations to the group in a simple, objective manner without creating defensiveness or confusion. He must be able to start the ball of evaluation discussion rolling in the group rather than "handing down the low-down." He must, of course, never use the role of observer as an opportunity to prove his superiority to the rest of the group or to be needlessly destructive.

Experience thus far has been with two types of observers. Certain participants with an interest in this type of function have been recruited ahead of time and been brought together for a preconference training session on observation techniques. In other conferences graduate students trained in clinical and group observation have been used. There are pros and cons for the use of each type. Participant observers, because of the short training period possible, are not so likely to have the skills of perceiving and interpreting that professionally trained group observers would have. On the other hand, there is the advantage that the participant observers are likely to have rather complete acceptance by their fellow participants. Furthermore, the very opportunity to learn and practice this function is a major asset which can carry over to their back-home jobs as well as become an asset in future

---

[1] Lippitt, R.; Bradford, L.; and Benne, K. "Sociodramatic Clarification of Leader and Group Roles as a Starting Point for Effective Group Functioning." *Sociatry;* March 1947.

NOTE: This article describes an orientation session with a spontaneous demonstration of leader and participant roles. The adaption of the observer role to such a demonstration can be readily imagined.

conferences and committees. With trained graduate students there is always the possibility that their youth can be taken as a point for resistance by certain participants who may feel on the defensive about the whole process of group self-assessment. If graduate students or other "trained outsiders" are to be used as group-process observers, they must be given careful training in the objectives of the conference and in the various angles of their working relationship with the participant group. They must be thoroughly sensitized to the problem of resistance to their youth or to the fact that they are "outsiders."

If participant observers are used, their training, brief as it is, becomes very important. Usually an afternoon and evening session just prior to the conference is utilized for the training of observers, leaders, and recorders. Observers learn to use a simple observation check list that guides their observation toward important clues of the group atmosphere, process and productivity growth, and group-member behavior. Shown on page 40 is one such check list used in a recent conference of professional workers.

A variety of such observation sheets have been developed. The most effective one for a particular conference will depend chiefly on the skills of the observers and on the amount of attention the conference group will want to put on analysis of group process.

The Postmeeting Suggestion Sheet

Practically all of us are happy to have an opportunity to "get off our chests" our feelings and reactions about meetings in which we participate. Usually this goes on informally in the lobby or the cloakroom. If it is channeled into an opportunity for regular anonymous suggestions and ratings at the end of each work-group meeting, it not only provides a constructive opportunity for the expression of these feelings but also serves as a major guidance to the group-discussion leader and to the group as a whole when all the ideas are put together and looked at as a basis for improving the productivity of the next meetings. Below is a typical postmeeting suggestion slip used in a number of conferences.

END-OF-MEETING SUGGESTION SLIP

What did you think of this meeting? Please be frank. Your comments can contribute a great deal both to the conference and to the profession. Our group observers will pool all the suggestions and summarize them for us.

1. How did you feel about this meeting? (Check)
   No good ☐ Mediocre ☐ All right ☐ Good ☐ Excellent ☐
2. What were the weaknesses?
3. What were the strong points?
4. What improvements would you suggest in the operations of the next meeting?

(Do not sign your name.)

Such postmeeting slips are collected by the observer, tabulated for each meeting, and reported back to the group.

The Feedback Role of the Observer

In a number of short work conferences the groups have found it most desirable to devote either the last 15 minutes of a 2- or 2-and-a-half-hour work session or a 10- or 15-minute observational review at the beginning of the second meeting to an assessment of their working productivity. Other longer conferences and workshops have found it even more productive to set aside certain special meeting periods as group-evaluation sessions, with the purpose of bringing about member growth and group improvement in work habits.

In the evaluation session the group-discussion leader turns the meeting over to the observer to begin with whatever observations he wishes to make. A skillful observer will very often offer only two or three symptoms he has observed in the group functioning and proffer a tentative hypothesis in question form about what the meaning of these symptoms might be. Such an hypothesis is usually sufficient to send the group off into a very constructive and nondefensive discussion. Very often in a first evaluation session the observer will start out with some observations about the leader role rather than about the group or any particular member roles. Because of their preconference training together, the leader is prepared to react objectively to the observer's comments and encouragingly to the role of the observer. Also, evaluation sessions are not seen as aggressively critical of members.

In addition to this function of "feeding back" data to the group about themselves for their own interpretation and reflection, the observer also functions as an important member of the leadership team with the discussion leader and the group recorder. During the conference these three frequently eat together to plan improvements in the discussion-leadership role and in the growth of the group. The successful working relationship of these three-person teams is really the heart of the success of a good work conference.

In our early explorations with conference process, the observation-feedback procedure was used only with the small work groups in the conference. When it became clear that the technique was so helpful in giving a sense of direction and progress and improvement in the small groups, it was decided to extend the idea to the total conference group also. Thus, in recent conferences it has become customary to have brief periods of the general conference sessions given over to a feed-back function. One successful pattern has been for the work-group content recorders to report to one coordinator at the end of the afternoon session and the process observers to report to a second co-ordinator. In these review sessions there would be a pooling of reports from all groups, and the co-ordinators would select certain themes of progress or of problems of progress. Each co-ordinator would then take 10 minutes in the general session in the evening to give an over-all report on conference achievement and conference problems of moving ahead more effectively as they were being met in the various work groups. Another procedure is to have a special conference spotter move around from one group to another and pull together his observations to give an over-all conference picture to the group in the general session. A third procedure is to have a panel of all the group recorders, or of all the group observers, meeting together in front of the general session. There is a very natural hunger for the participants in all the groups to know what is going on in other groups and certainly a great opportunity for one group to profit by the problems other groups are meeting and the successes they are having.

At this stage of the development of conference procedure it is safe to predict that 10 years from now a typical professional conference will utilize a wide variety of techniques to stimulate and maintain its own creative productivity. We are on the edge of a great vista of new developments in working together as creative human beings.

Staging Behavioral Science Learning Experience: Transforming Observers into Participants

SAMUEL A. CULBERT and
WARREN H. SCHMIDT

The techniques described in this article would transform observers attending a presentation on group dynamics into learning participants. The resistances of the audience to learning about self—and in public—are met with nine strategies or "Guidelines for Audience Involvement" devised by the behavioral scientist authors. In the language of the legitimate stage, observers fill participant roles under a competent director who bars the critics and utilizes a good script and a large cast.

Among the many roles the behavioral science educator is asked to fill, one seems to stand out as most difficult: it is the role of featured program speaker presenting a behavioral science approach to individual effectiveness in groups and organizations. In filling this role the behavioral science educator makes a number of key assumptions about learning which conflict strongly with the beliefs typically held by his audience. These conflicts make for difficult educating assignments and challenge behavioral scientists to invent new educating techniques. Optimally, these techniques should allow a behavioral scientist to educate in a style that is consistent with his own assumptions about how people learn best while at the same time showing respect for the concerns and resist-

Reprinted by special permission from THE JOURNAL OF APPLIED BE-
HAVIORAL SCIENCE, Volume 5, Number 3.

ances which are generated by the assumptions of his audience. The exposition of a framework for resolving these conflicts is the topic of this paper.

Typically, a behavioral scientist receives a telephone call from the convention chairman of a volunteer organization requesting that he make a presentation at their annual convention. The program chairman says, "We will have a group of about 200 leaders of our organization at this conference. They need to know about groups and how they operate. We have set aside an hour and a half to two hours for such a presentation on group dynamics. Can you help us?"

Frequently involved in this kind of request is a characteristic role conflict perceived by the behavioral scientist. On the one hand, he realizes that this is an opportunity for a strategic group of people to gain some exposure to behavioral science concepts which have important application value. He is aware of the fact that significant learnings about group behavior inevitably involve learnings about self and, therefore, require a high degree of participation and involvement of the audience. On the other hand, he is aware of the educational problems posed by the fact that he must deal with a large group of people in a short space of time, and that they will probably come expecting a lecture. One question with which he may wrestle is this: "Can I provide a meaningful learning experience for this number of people in this short space of time?" He is also likely to become sharply aware of how his beliefs and expectations may differ from the beliefs and expectations of his audience. Juxtaposed the differences are these:

The Behavioral Science Educator believes	*The Audience believes*
Knowledge is not behavior. Improving one's effectiveness in groups involves much more than learning new terms and concepts.	Improving my competence in groups is like learning about anything else. If I learn *the* guiding principles which apply I shall be a better leader.
In improving one's functioning, the person must first recognize his own style of behavior and the attitudes, beliefs, and personal assumptions underlying it.	There is an objective body of knowledge — a set of rules which work, regardless of the person applying them.

The Behavioral Science
Educator believes   *The Audience believes*

Personal experience and analysis must precede conceptualization of learnings. Therefore, the learner must *first* become an active participant.

The learner's responsibility is to listen to the conceptualizations of the expert. In that way the learner will become more expert himself and later will be able to apply the learnings.

To take a fresh look at these ideas, it is necessary to generate behavior which can be viewed by many individuals so that the learner can be freer of personally determined conceptions and distortions.

To test any theory ask:
1. Does it fit my past experience?
2. Does it show me ways to solve the practical problems, as *I* see them, about me?

The above comparison and contrast portrays the experience-based learning assumptions made by the behavioral scientist and illustrates two major sources of audience resistance to the kind of program he would like to provide. These two sources are (a) resistance to learning about the self—with all of its implications of threat, recognition of inadequacy, need to change, and so on; (b) resistance to a learning experience requiring the public display of behavior—with all of its implications for embarrassment, exposure to criticism, and so on. The text which follows will bring into focus some of the concerns represented by these resistances and suggest strategies and techniques which behavioral science educators might use in coping with them.

Resistances to Experience-Based Learning About Self

Any kind of self-learning entails risks since it involves an openness to confronting one's own vulnerabilities and needs to change. Few are eager to risk discovering that they have misinterpreted the meaning of past experiences, that they lack the insight to fully understand current experiences, or that they lack the ability to carry out certain personal tasks effectively. The risk in self-learning is even more apparent when the learning deals with performance in interpersonal relationships, leadership roles, groups, and so on—topics on which the learner is well experienced and on which he believes others have high expectations for him to be competent. Thus, when people are confronted with learning situations dealing

with such topics they usually find it easier to look for gim-
micks and objective principles than to become more aware of
their own limitations as instruments for learning.

These natural resistances to learning about self are intensi-
fied in large meetings which have an audience participation
format. Here the participant may feel particularly vulnerable
because such contexts expose personal assumptions and behavior to scrutiny by others as well as by one's self. In the
face of such vulnerabilities and concerns over possible criticism, it is natural for people to develop defenses against having their behavior critiqued by others. In a large meeting
these defenses may appear as well-established "learning
games." The following participant thoughts and assumptions
are characteristic of some of these games.

- You're the expert. Make your subject interesting and applicable to my problems, or I'll be free to criticize you.
- That may work in theory, but you don't understand my
  problem.
- Give me the principles, and I'll decide whether or not they
  fit.
- I'll interpret your statements so that they support what I
  want to do.
- If somebody challenges what I'm doing, I'll say it was your
  idea.

The experience-based model of self-learning squarely con-
fronts these learning games. This model proceeds along the
very format against which learning games have been formulated to defend. While learning games represent, in part at
least, participant resistances to becoming actively involved in
a learning experience and assuming responsibility for the
quality of that learning, the experience-based format attempts
to place this responsibility with the individual learner. For
this reason the experience-based model always arouses audience concerns when introduced as a program format. Moreover, classed as a form of learning by participation, resistances to experience-based methods are often supported in the
minds of the audience members by their past experiences in
conference participation. They may recall discussion groups
which were poorly led, workgroups which degenerated into
unproductive bull sessions, and similar group experiences
which in relying on unstructured participation by groups from
the audience were unexciting and relatively unproductive.

The feelings of the audience might be summarized thus: "I came here to learn from somebody who *knows* something, not to talk with a bunch of amateurs." In behaving as if they believed that all group experiences are loosely organized, lack expert direction, and have doubtful potential for productivity, prospective participants are able to use past experiences to cloak whatever personal concerns they are presently experiencing around their own participation. This objection is not readily forgotten and is frequently brought up whether the learning situation is loosely conceptualized or is presented as a well-conceptualized, experience-based format with assurances to participants of direction and organization.

How can a behavioral science educator (a "consultant" in this context) cope with these resistances and reduce the likelihood that the audience (or "clients") will engage in playing these unproductive learning games? Of course the consultant must remember to communicate the organization and direction of his program. But chiefly he must find a way to help set new expectations and make it comfortable for his client(s) to move from a passive to an active role. In some ways this is analogous to moving a person from the seat he took in the audience to the position of an actor on the stage—to move him from the role of an "observer" into the role of a "participant." We have found this analogy useful in highlighting both the dynamics and the methods required in assisting potential participants to move beyond their personal concerns so that they may accept and experiment with the assumptions of experience-based learning.

How to Get Actors Onstage

There are many more risks entailed in being an actor onstage than in remaining an observer in the audience. In addition to many personal factors, these risks are a function of the probability of a performance failure and the costs the client sees in failure. Such costs are often experienced as feelings of inadequacy, incompetence, embarrassment, or shame. The behavioral science educator can offer help with these risks by attempting to assist the participant both to increase the probability of a good performance and to lower the cost of a poor performance. At this point it is recommended that the consultant offer some assurance that he has the resources to perform competently as director of the learning experience for the client. Initially the behavioral science consultant is seen only as a polished actor, and participants require some behavioral demonstration to broaden their expectations of him to include some confidence that the consultant can also direct them in a successful performance. The consultant might lead the way by sharing assumptions which he believes the participants make about their potential to perform and by mentioning the things he intends to do to help them. In addition, the consultant can increase the incentives to perform by highlighting the potential learning to be gained in a performance.

Perhaps the best way to ensure that participants will agree to "get into the act" is by not allowing them enough time to get settled into the posture of a safe, secure audience. Early participation is recommended. Such participation should be aimed at providing a success experience, i.e., a genuine, bona fide piece of experience-based learning. In producing successful performances, the consultant may with justification sacrifice breadth of learning for safety: he recognizes that he has only a short amount of time and that the safe learning experience is really but the first step on a three-step learning progression.

Although the next two steps are not the focus of this paper, they are, second, a learning situation that is less structured and controlled, entails greater client risk, and leaves more responsibility with the client; and third, learning from everyday experiences in the client's natural environment. For instance, the first step—a safe, somewhat limited learning exercise—might be structured as an hour-and-a-half sensitivity training microlab. The second step—less structured, less controlled, and with more client risk and client responsibility—might be a follow-up, two-week residential laboratory. On the third step, the client would take full responsibility for transferring his laboratory learning and making back-home applications.

Participant Concerns and Program Strategies

Thanks to educational innovations and experiments of the past 25 years, the behavioral scientist now has a wide range of strategies and techniques to facilitate active audience involvement. These generally serve to reduce participants' anxieties and concerns so that they are freer to concentrate on the learning experience. We have summarized these strategies and techniques in nine "Guidelines for Audience Involvement" described in the following paragraphs and shown in

Figure 1. Each Guideline is expressed in the language of stagecraft and is linked to a particular participant concern, together with its expected consequences.

1. PARTICIPANT CONCERN: *"Can I be confident that I'll learn something?"*

    INVOLVEMENT TECHNIQUE: *Share the production cost (by sharing the knowledge that the director is competent).*

This concern is always present among members of an audience, but it is accentuated in a setting where people are expected to participate actively. They want to be sure that their investment of energy will, indeed, result in greater learning. This puts a heavier responsibility on the program presenter to state clearly the objectives of the program, the plan for achieving these objectives, and the rationale for participation. He must make clear that the program has been planned carefully. He is inviting the members of the audience to *join* with him in an exciting adventure in learning, and it is important that they see it in this way.

2. PARTICIPANT CONCERN: *"I am not an actor or a talker."*

    INVOLVEMENT TECHNIQUE: *Provide a low stage (on which it is comfortable to perform).*

Most people are self-conscious in a large-group setting. Relatively few feel comfortable expressing themselves while several hundred persons observe them. The task of the program presenter is to reduce this kind of anxiety as quickly as possible by helping the participant to engage in a more informal small-group experience. This can be done by having each member of the audience talk with the person next to him briefly about some experience in a successful or unsuccessful group. It can be accomplished by setting up buzz groups at appropriate times. Participation in a small group with a clearly defined focus of discussion provides a kind of "low stage" which makes participation seem easy and comfortable.

3. PARTICIPANT CONCERN: *"I know it already and wonder whether it is worth my time to learn it again."*

    INVOLVEMENT TECHNIQUE: *Change sets (to give fresh perspective).*

People bring to behavioral science many theories of their own. The presenter of a program about group behavior can assume that many members of his audience have already made up their minds about whether groups are useful or not, what the leader should do to make a group effective, and what causes groups to fail. The average participant's experience has led him to many "common sense" theories about group behavior which he may be reluctant to examine critically. The challenge to the program presenter is to provide a setting in which the participant can take a fresh look at his assumptions in the light of his experiences. This can be done by using some kind of paper-and-pencil instrument which calls for him to respond in a way that projects his assumptions and theories. It can be done by asking him to observe a role-playing situation and to share his analysis of its dynamics with other members of the audience. Basically, the goal is to help the participant produce some response which he can compare with the responses of other members of the audience exposed to the same situation. In this way he has a chance to get his own thinking into a fresh perspective.

4. PARTICIPANT CONCERN: *"Can I 'get hurt' if I make mistakes or look inept?"*

INVOLVEMENT TECHNIQUE: *Bar the critics.*

Action learning requires a person to produce behavior which may expose weaknesses. There is a natural reluctance to exhibit one's ignorance, bias, or clumsiness if such exposure will later be used against him. The program presenter must therefore ensure that participants feel secure and that they do not have to worry about making mistakes in the learning process. The program presenter should not ask people to do things beyond their capacities; there should be a well-established ground rule which prevents the kind of criticism which is damaging to the ego. If participants are asked to respond to some instrument, their data should be handled anonymously or kept under their own control. Similarly, the device of role playing provides a kind of protective shell for persons expected to perform for the whole group. Procedures which make it possible for a person to rationalize misbehavior if he finds it necessary to do so should always be provided.

5. PARTICIPANT CONCERN: *"What am I supposed to say and do?"*

INVOLVEMENT TECHNIQUE: *Provide a good script.*

People know how to behave as a passive audience; but when they are asked to participate, they want clear direction.

For the program presenter this means defining clearly the first action steps the individual is to take. He should also provide time for participants to "get into role" and to obtain whatever information is necessary before they are expected to produce behavior. If the opening actions (scenes) are clear, meaningful, and lead to success, the participant's own sense of security and adequacy will increase and he will be a more effective learner.

6. PARTICIPANT CONCERN: *"Will I know how to proceed?"*

INVOLVEMENT TECHNIQUE: *Provide necessary props (to give support and direction).*

Many participants will have some anxiety about getting into a situation in which they might become confused, uncertain, or embarrassed. Their concern is analogous to that of an actor who worries about forgetting his lines at a critical moment. Here the task of the program presented is to provide a supportive environment where the necessary tools are available at the time when they are needed. If the program calls for a simulated committee meeting, it is helpful to have the chairs and table in place and briefing sheets for the role players. If a participant is expected to observe the simulated meeting from certain points of view, it helps to provide him with a form which readily categorizes his observations. The presence of these materials (props) not only demonstrates that the program is well planned but gives the participant a sense of continuing support in his learning effort.

7. PARTICIPANT CONCERN: *"People may laugh at me, and I'll be embarrassed."*

INVOLVEMENT TECHNIQUE: *Employ a large cast (to avoid making the participants feel conspicuous and alone).*

This is but another expression of a natural fear of showing weakness and inadequacy and is related to the reluctance to perform in front of a large group. The challenge to the program presenter is to reduce this anxiety by helping each person to feel less alone, isolated, and conspicuous. By having the total audience engaged in the same activity, each individual can blend into the background as much as he wishes. He can feel that his mistakes will not be highlighted, because others are also busy performing.

8. PARTICIPANT CONCERN: *"How much responsibility am I expected to carry?"*
INVOLVEMENT TECHNIQUE: *Make it a dress rehearsal (to emphasize practice).*

It is one thing to be a good member of a passive audience; it is quite another to feel personal responsibility for the quality of a learning experience. As the program presenter nudges the audience in the latter direction, he must be sure that he does not overemphasize the burden of responsibility which each participant must carry. He must make clear that perfection is not required to make this a useful experience. By underscoring the fact that the goal is to *learn* rather than to demonstrate competence he will reduce the tendency of the participant to be overcritical of self and others.

9. PARTICIPANT CONCERN: *"If I make a mistake, others will see me and I'll look incompetent."*
INVOLVEMENT TECHNIQUE: *Dim the houselights (and provide some anonymity).*

In the face of such expressions of anxiety and fear of criticism, the program presenter can here set a climate of safety where the views of observers are less important than the personal views of the participant himself. He can place an emphasis on each participant as one who behaves rather than as one who observes. If some instrument is used, for example, which shows a participant how much or how little he knows about a given subject, he should not be pressed to share the results with others. Sensitive data, provided anonymously, are likely to be much more useful during initial learning experiences than data with which the participant must identify publicly.

SUMMARY

Learning about human relations is seldom a passive task. It requires active involvement by the learner—a sense of quest and willingness to look analytically at his own feelings and behavior. Human relations learning also requires the building of trust and time for the learner to reflect.

Few program occasions provide an audience that expects involvement, built-in opportunities for the program presenter to develop trusting relationships, or sufficient time for the audience members to reflect on their learnings. Yet these occasions are opportunities for the exposure of new groups to the insights of behavioral science.

The behavioral scientist who is invited to be the key figure in such a program faces a dilemma that tests his creativity and skill. He must fulfill audience expectations for learning by using procedures they do not expect. He must, in effect, rewrite his contract with them while seeking to gain sufficient trust that they will risk with him. He must transform passive observers into active performers within a short space of time. He must give those who participate the opportunity to relate their experiences to behavioral science concepts. And while providing a rewarding experience, he must leave that sense of incompleteness which leads the participant to seek richer and deeper experiences.

Guidelines for Audience Involvement

Participant Concerns	Strategy	"Stage" Technique	Consequences
Can I be confident that I'll learn something?	Make clear that program has been carefully planned to achieve useful outcomes; participation is essential to achieve these.	Share the production cost.	1) Reduces psychological distance between resource person and participants 2) Makes learning easier because of shared risk and investment 3) Avoids feeling that "we have been left on our own."
I am not an actor or a talker.	Use a natural activity in moving participants toward learning objectives.	Use a low stage.	1) Easy to participate 2) Nonthreatening 3) First actions are easy and require no advance preparation.
I know it already and wonder whether it is worth my time to learn it again.	Put it in a new context so that former learning patterns are not repeated.	Change sets.	1) Gives a fresh look at things 2) Circumvents old learning blocks 3) Stimulates new ideas for application
This is artificial.			4) Helps develop "play-acting" spirit, i.e., an unreal world in which the cost of failure is low.
Can I "get hurt" if I make mistakes or look inept?	Either limit admission to the audience or provide reassurance that given this audience we are not	Bar the critics.	1) Makes it "safer" to admit weaknesses and imperfections 2) Reduces defensiveness and anxiety

Guidelines for Audience Involvement—*continued*

Participant Concerns	Strategy	"Stage" Technique	Consequences
	going to ask you to do anything that should hurt you.		3) Increases the ability to look at one's own behavior, analyze it, and learn from it.
What am I supposed to say and do?	Guide behavior in productive, meaningful direction.	*Provide a good script.*	1) Persons are helped to "get into role." 2) Security about what to do is provided; a sense of direction is given. 3) Early experience of success is more likely. 4) Gives a polished look to the performance.
Will I know how to proceed?	Augment the quality of performance by providing professional props. Anticipate client needs and eliminate concerns which detract from the participant's concentration.	*Provide necessary props.*	1) Helps develop "play-acting" spirit, i.e., an unreal world in which the cost of failure is low 2) Demonstrates that program is well planned 3) Demonstrates that the program staff is really concerned with productivity.
People may laugh at me and I'll be embarrassed.	Help participant be as inconspicuous as he wishes to be while taking part.	*Employ a large cast.*	1) Mistakes will not be noticed or highlighted. 2) Supports feeling of not being alone. 3) "We're all in the same boat" (shared risk). 4) Reduces self-consciousness.
How much responsibility am I expected to carry?	Increase atmosphere of practice rather than performance.	*Make it a dress rehearsal.*	1) Clarifies goal as learning rather than demonstrating competence 2) Reduces tendency to be overly critical of self and others.
If I make a mistake, others will see me and I'll look incompetent.	Increase permissiveness and tolerance for differences of behavior.	*Dim the houselights.*	1) Observers are less conspicuous. 2) Reactions of observers are less distracting. 3) Emphasis is on each participant as a producer of behavior rather than as an observer.

Evaluating the Effectiveness of Meetings

RICHARD BECKHARD

Every person, either consciously or unconsciously, evaluates every meeting of which he is a part. What we do not always do, however, is evaluate systematically, using all the information available to find out how we are doing and where improvements can be made.

One of the important things that has developed recently, in terms of evaluation of meetings, is a concept of evaluation different from that which we used previously. Evaluation is seen now as an integral part of the process of planning a meeting rather than as something which takes place after the event. If we can get more facts and fewer hunches as we go along in our planning, we will improve the effectiveness of our meetings.

There are several places where evaluation is critically important:

1. At the initial planning
2. When firming up the program plan
3. At the meeting
4. After the meeting.

Initial Planning

Let us look first at number one—the initial planning. Every meeting has a number of stated objectives. These may include exchanging experiences, conducting business, receiving new

Reprinted by special permission of the JOURNAL OF THE AMERICAN TRADE ASSOCIATION EXECUTIVES (now the JOURNAL OF THE AMERICAN SOCIETY OF ASSOCIATION EXECUTIVES) and of the author.

information, solving problems, setting policy, and so on. In addition to these stated objectives, there are a number of unstated objectives which are equally important and must be dealt with if the meeting is to pay off. One might be that some people come to the meeting to see friends, change jobs, or do any number of things that do not relate directly to the business at hand. This is part of one category of objectives—members' objectives. Another category is the objectives of the planners themselves. In addition, there are the organization's objectives—the policies that must be decided upon, the business that must be transacted. Then there are the officers' personal objectives—to appear on the platform, deliver an address, be re-elected, and so on. The planner must find ways of integrating these several sets of purposes in such a way that the organizational goals will be met, insofar as possible, in terms that are meaningful to all individuals concerned.

Here is an example of how one organization used such information in its planning. A group of manufacturers in the Midwest had stated as their objective the conducting of a series of monthly meetings on management. The *planners'* objective was to have this group become acquainted with a certain area of scientific management. The *officers'* objective was to initiate a kind of series that would be different from any they had had before—one with more participation and with much heavier attendance. The *organization's* objective was total organizational improvement. In order to find out the *members'* objectives in this particular subject (which happened to be human relations training), a questionnaire was sent to all the membership. They were asked what types of training programs they had, how many people were in the company, how many people took training, and so on. From these questionnaires the planners could see what the members' problems were, as the members themselves saw them. The first thing that was done at the meeting was to show the entire membership how the agenda had been developed from their questionnaire responses. Also, it should be noted, this device of involving the members prior to the meeting increased the attendance by close to 10 percent.

A second area where evaluation is critical is at the point of finalizing the program plan and setting the methods of presentation and whatever audience-participation methods are to be used. Here again, it is important to have a systematic procedure for determining which presentation method and which audience technique to use. Each single item of subject material on a program should be related to these two questions:

1. What is the nature of the material (technical, philosophical, statistical, controversial)?
2. What is the situation in which it will be presented (activities that precede it and follow it, level of audience interest in subject, level of audience familiarity with subject)?

Answers to these questions will almost automatically determine preferences in presentation method and will help to determine audience-participation procedures.

Evaluation Techniques

Here cited is an illustration of how an insurance association used evaluation techniques to change its schedule: The tentative program plan for a three-day meeting called for the conference to open with a series of concurrent "bull sessions" on different subjects—14 or 15 of them, with experts on a particular subject located in each room. The members could shop in the "cafeteria" of subjects and could come and go as they pleased. This activity was to take up the first morning. The plan called for the first general session that afternoon.

As the planners analyzed the plan in terms of the two criteria—*kind of material* and *situation in which it is being presented*—they felt that the dispersal of the whole group in a series of meetings as a *first* activity would establish a diffuse climate rather than a feeling of belonging. They also knew that members like to spend the first morning locating friends, arranging golf foursomes, and the like. As this technique would make such activity extremely difficult, they changed the schedule to put the general session in the morning and the bull sessions in the afternoon. As simple as this may sound, they probably would not have made the decision to change the schedule unless they had had a systematic method of evaluating their plan as they went along.

Postmeeting Procedure

More familiar to all of us is the systematic evaluation that takes place at the meeting and after the meeting. Because there are several kinds of evaluation that can be used, planners should determine to what purpose the evaluation is to be directed. Basically there are two categories of facts collected at a meeting: the first category is *facts for steering purposes*—this would include reactions of a group that was meeting several times. Such facts can guide the discussion leader in his planning and can aid in the day-by-day evaluations of a conference as guidance for a steering committee. The other major category is *facts for future planning*. This category includes end-of-the-meeting reactions and reactions taken at a later date—after the members are back home.

The first category of evaluation—for steering purposes—may be performed in a number of ways. A short evaluation form, sometimes called a postmeeting reaction form, can be distributed at the end of each session. It would ask such questions as these: How did you feel about this session (very good, good, all right, not good)? How helpful was this session? Why? What do you think the group ought to do next?

Periodic Interviews

A selected sample of members can be interviewed at periodic intervals, say, once a day. Another device is to select an evaluation team which more or less systematically conducts hallway interviews and reports its findings to some central source at periodic intervals.

All of these techniques also provide useful information for the second category of evaluation—for future planning. In addition, planners usually need to know the answers to the following questions to guide them in future planning:

1. What did the members expect and hope for from the meeting?
2. How well did the meeting meet their expectations and hopes?
3. What gaps in information, experience, and so on, did the members see as unfilled?
4. How useful did the members consider the meeting?
5. What were members' opinions on the subject matter chosen?
6. What were members' opinions on the presentation methods used?
7. How well did the members feel that *their* problems were dealt with?
8. What use, if any, do members plan to make of material from the meeting?

Attitude Measurements

This information can be obtained best at the end of the meeting, or at a time subsequent to the meeting, or both. If you want to measure change in attitude, such as how well a meeting met member expectations, you will probably want to take before- and after-meeting measurements. The same would be true of how members used the material at the meeting. One large association with an attendance of about 10,000 persons at its annual convention and trade show secures this information in this way:

Each member of a selected sample of about 300 persons, representing every category of member attending and with geographic and functional representation, is given a brief questionnaire which is placed in his hotel mail box upon his arrival. He is asked to fill this out and return it immediately to the home office in an enclosed envelope. In the same packet there is another envelope (sealed). He is asked to fill out the second questionnaire at the end of the convention and to mail it also to the home office.

These two devices give a picture of how well the program met expectations and how a sampling of persons felt about it. Another selected sample is given a questionnaire at the end of the meeting (this is comparable to the end-of-the-meeting questionnaire given to the first sample). The second group is sent another questionnaire 90 days after the meeting which is designed to find out how members are using the material from the convention—how they have revised their opinions given at the end of the meeting—and what, in the light of their further back-home experience, they would like to see on next year's program.

Information Helpful

The administration of these four questionnaires is not an especially arduous job, and the organization has found that the information received from them has been a major factor in planning future programs and in predicting the acceptance of the programs by the members.

Each meeting planner must find the kinds of evaluation procedures that are economically and functionally practical for his meetings. However, regardless of procedures used, all planners can improve the effectiveness of their planning and the consequent effectiveness of their meetings by building into their planning procedures systematic ways of appraising the situation as they go along, with particular emphasis on the four critical points of initial planning—the programming, the selection of presentation methods, the meeting itself, and the postmeeting phase.

SECTION III

SPECIAL

CONFERENCES

The Fact-Finding
Conference

WARREN H. SCHMIDT and
RICHARD BECKHARD

An Analysis of Different Types of Conferences

The conference, as a medium of communication and as a setting for problem solving, decision making, planning, and idea sharing, is a major activity for all who work in organizations or in communities. Nearly all such persons aspire to improve their efficiency in using the conference medium, since it represents such a large investment of time.

In recent years, social scientists have studied the problems of communication, and adult educators have refined the methods and techniques of communication. This research and experimentation has pointed up the fact that conferences are complex and require careful and systematic planning if they are to produce results.

It has also become apparent that there are different types of conferences and that each type has different kinds of results.

You are probably familiar with three types of conferences: information-giving, problem-solving, and information-exchange. This monograph introduces a fourth kind: the *fact-finding* or *exploratory* conference. The differences between the first three types and the fact-finding conference are discussed below.

Reprinted from THE FACT-FINDING CONFERENCE by Warren H. Schmidt and Richard Beckhard by special permission of the Adult Education Association of the United States and of the authors.

THE INFORMATION-GIVING CONFERENCE

As the name implies, the unique characteristic of the information-giving conference is that the planners present information to the conference participants. Action or problem solving stimulated by such a conference occurs after the conference is over and is likely to differ for different participants. It is likely that there will be no group consensus called for on anything. If a community defense director called together representatives of various agencies to tell them about the state-wide civil defense plan, it would be unrealistic for him to hope for any group action at the conference. Any action would have to be taken subsequently, either individually or at another and different kind of conference.

THE PROBLEM-SOLVING OR DECISION-MAKING CONFERENCE

The problem-solving or decision-making conference is designed to obtain group agreement or action on some problem, issue, or policy. The convener definitely expects to get decisions made or problems solved at the meeting. If, for example, the participants in the civil defense meeting mentioned above had gone back to their agencies and called conferences to decide how they might participate in a community program, these meetings would be decision-making conferences. The outcome hoped for would be a plan of action which the agency could carry out.

THE INFORMATION-EXCHANGE CONFERENCE

In the information-exchange conference, participants need information *from one another* rather than from the convener or an outside source. The convener's objective in this case is to provide a setting where such exchange of experience can take place. It is assumed that the participants have previously decided that it will be useful to spend time in this manner. The participants in an information-exchange conference are seen as resource people. The convener usually serves as a resource person as well as a discussion leader. To follow our illustration, a group of agencies might hold an information-exchange conference to compare notes on what each of them was doing to further the civil defense program. The information-exchange conference does not require group agreement or action, although they sometimes occur as by-products.

THE FACT-FINDING CONFERENCE

The distinguishing characteristic of the fact-finding conference is that its *primary* objective is to get from the participants information and opinions which will form the basis
for future planning and action. In this type of meeting, the
participants again are chosen because of their resources.
Although action is often a by-product of the fact-finding
conference, the objectives of the meeting are attained even
if the group does not arrive at agreement or commitment
to action.

If our civil defense official had convened representatives
of the various agencies in his community to find out what
their attitudes were toward the civil defense program and
what steps they thought were needed—all this as a basis
for a governmental decision regarding how much staff and
budget would be allocated to this community—such a convening would be a fact-finding conference. The convener
would be collecting information from the participants.

Two of the situations in which the fact-finding conference
can produce significant results are—

1. Within an organization.
    (a) Periodic conferences by national staff with regional
        or state leaders
    (b) Assessment by state staff or leaders of needs and
        problems at community level
    (c) Periodic reporting by field staff to headquarters staff
    (d) Visits by national staff to local communities
    (e) Determination of needs, problems, and attitudes of
        staff who are several levels lower.

One president of an industrial concern, for example, holds
a fact-finding conference with each group of first-line supervisors once a year. He receives a great deal of information,
but does not disturb the relationship between these men and
their immediate supervisors, since the conference is for information and not action. These conferences have had a
significant effect on morale.

2. Among organizations.
    (a) Exploratory meetings to determine needs for co-
        operative or coordinated activity in a particular field,
        at the local, state, regional, or national level

(b) Meetings of groups of interested leaders to explore facts on a particular community problem

(c) Fact-finding about professional standards in a particular field

(d) Identification of gaps in services by representatives of agencies.

One hazard in convening a fact-finding conference is that the planning group sometimes has purposes in mind other than the stated ones. The fact-finding conference is misused if it is convened for the primary purpose of easing a reluctant group into some kind of action. An analogy might be the type of magazine salesman who begins his sales pitch by pretending to conduct a survey on reading habits. The planner probably ought *not* to convene a fact-finding conference unless he believes—

1. That there are problems in which the participants have common interests and about which they have experience.

2. That if these common interests and the information about the problem are made known, the group will be capable of deciding whether any action is appropriate.

3. That the planner's responsibility is essentially to create a situation in which the relevant information and experience can come into the open. He assumes no responsibility for subsequent action of the group.

When a planning group feels that some kind of action is desirable, it is well to indicate this impression in the letters of invitation. This calls for a different type of conference, however. In this case the planner says, in effect, "Some of us feel that there is a need for this committee to begin some concerted action along these lines. We are asking those people who have ideas and opinions about this problem to come together and examine the feasibility of joint efforts to deal with it." Such a conference moves closer to becoming a problem-solving than a fact-finding conference. There is an implication that the group is to make decisions. This poses certain problems, particularly when the participants are selected because they represent different organizations or segments of the community. Participants will tend to be more cautious in expressing ideas when they feel that they are making or implying commitments for the groups they represent.

Ten Features of the Fact-Finding Conference

In order to know when to use the fact-finding conference to obtain subsequent positive action, it is necessary to know why conferences called to collect information produce other effects. We have isolated 10 features of the fact-finding conference that seem instrumental in producing the results obtained.

> 1. *The Fact-Finding Conference Can Bring Together People Who Would Not Come Together Otherwise*

No commitment is required, making it possible for individuals whose organizations or departments or agencies are seen as rivals and competitors to participate without compromising their organizational loyalties. Representatives of management and labor, of agricultural extension and public schools, of professional and lay groups, of different staff levels, and of many other divergent groups can participate in fact-finding conferences, even if they have different approaches and despite the fact that some of them may view the programs of others with dismay and suspicion.

> 2. *The Fact-Finding Conference Provides a Comfortable Setting in Which To Express Ideas and Attitudes*

The participant knows he will not be required to "take a stand" on anything or officially endorse any plan of action. He is not viewed as an official representative of his organization, so no one expects him to defend the group to which he belongs. He simply is to report and describe his group's program and problems, not to impress or defend. The fact-finding purpose of the meeting encourages information giving and objectivity rather than comparison and evaluation.

> 3. *The Fact-Finding Conference Helps To Clear Up Misunderstandings*

Misunderstandings result partly from lack of information and/or lack of communication. The fact-finding conference is uniquely equipped to resolve misunderstandings. Problems of relationships between agencies or individuals do not become *issues* for resolution at the meeting, but are presented as informational items. They are not discussed in the context of "who is to blame," but rather as obstacles to achieving common goals.

4. The Fact-Finding Conference Establishes Many New Informal Channels of Communication Among Participants

Individuals attending the conference get to know one another and to see who is associated with various organizations. Since no participant is acting as an official representative of his group, a situation exists in which *personal* relationships can be established more easily. The result is that when an executive of one organization or the head of one department or branch needs to make contact with some other group later on, he has a personal contact. Thus, even though no official relationships have been established between the two organizations or departments, an informal liaison has been created which is likely to make each more useful to the other.

5. The Fact-Finding Conference Produces More Information and Insights than Are Possible Through Other Survey Methods

Surveys and other media do not provide the stimulation and interaction necessary to help people to identify basic issues and develop new insights. Often the most important information about organizations in a community exists only in the minds and feelings of people, and this kind of information is difficult to list on a questionnaire form. Sometimes such information is also difficult to report to an interviewer. However, in a setting in which one idea "triggers off" another, a bit of information which might have remained hidden comes out. It is doubtful whether anyone could devise an interview schedule that could elicit the kind of information about interpersonal and interorganizational relationships that emerges in the fact-finding conference.

6. The Fact-Finding Conference Stimulates Follow-Up Action Growing Out of Real Needs

Because such a conference has no stated *action* goal, the group is free to spend more time in diagnosing problems. Any plan that develops must clearly grow out of needs and problems felt by the entire group. There is less chance that the group will push for action for action's sake. By contrast, conferences set up specifically for problem-solving or planning purposes sometimes press participants to make action decisions before they have adequately diagnosed problems or obtained facts.

7. The Fact-Finding Conference Paves the Way for Co-Operative Action

The experience of looking together at community needs and analyzing them helps develop a sense of unity. Staff members who have a day-to-day responsibility for preparing programs learn to know other individuals in the community who share similar objectives and face similar problems. When problems of common concern are brought out by a fact-finding conference, it is only a short step to ask, 'What can we do *together* to deal with these problems?"

8. The Fact-Finding Conference Enables Participants To Understand More Fully the Objectives, Boundaries, and Problems of Other Organizations

In this setting, information about organizations is usually looked upon as *objective*. Every organization has certain limitations and points of emphasis in its program, and it is helpful to other groups to know what these limitations and emphases are so that there can be a better understanding among groups in a community. In a fact-finding conference this kind of information is regarded as factual; evaluation is out of bounds. The *ad hoc* conference group obviously has no power to change the existing boundaries, and so the discussion is limited to analysis rather than recommendation.

9. The Fact-Finding Conference Is Rewarding to the Individual Participant

The setting of the fact-finding conference gives each participant a good opportunity to make new acquaintances, to develop better feelings of understanding and better relationships with other key people in the community. There is also greater freedom and encouragement to participate than many organizational leaders usually encounter. Since no one is an official representative, each participant can express himself quite freely. For example, in this setting, the labor leader need not represent labor, but can react to community problems as a citizen who has a certain background of experience. The same is true of the teacher, the Chamber of Commerce executive, the YMCA secretary, the regional director, the foreman, and so on. In general, participants at fact-finding conferences find the experience a pleasant and rewarding one.

10. The Fact-Finding Conference Produces an Unusually Good Setting for Creative Thinking

Many of the pressures which tend to inhibit creative thinking are absent—defensiveness, threat, criticism, and pressure to reach a decision in a limited time. The effort to diagnose problems at as deep a level as possible tends to suggest new patterns of relationships and new kinds of activities. Experience indicates that the group will tend to go further than the superficial identification of problems and will concern themselves with basic issues. When this occurs, the way is open for new and creative approaches to long-standing issues.

While many of these features may characterize other types of conferences, the combination of features seems to occur more readily in the fact-finding meeting. One reason for this is the way the fact-finding conference is planned.

Designing a Work Conference on Change and Problem Solving

W. WARNER BURKE and
BETTY R. ELLIS

In recent years behavioral scientists have been asked to help formulate designs for conferences or workshops on change. Almost inevitably, change, be it technological or social, creates problems. As a result, many institutions and organizations are presently conducting, or planning to conduct, a conference on solving some of the problems concerning one or more of the many complex issues which face our society. Due to the immediacy of need and, often, the limited time which organizations have available, these conferences have to be designed for a short period of time, i.e., one-three days. Based on the authors' experience with brief work conferences, this article concerns some of the necessary ingredients for a successful conference focused on change and problem solving.

As conceptualized in the design of this type of conference, problem solving is envisioned as involving two processes. The first process is that of designing the format of the conference itself. This design follows the sequential steps of the problem-solving process which behavioral scientists have found to be quite effective. The second process is that of establishing a "climate for work." A conducive "climate" or attitude of mind for work with one another is critical for problems to be solved. This climate involves the acquisition of a highly trained and qualified staff, adequate facilities, a preconference training and planning period, money (of all things), as well as other factors. What follows is a description of these two integral processes.

117

Reprinted by special permission of ADULT LEADERSHIP and of the author.

The Problem-Solving Process As the Basis
for a Conference Design

Based on research evidence as well as experience in laboratory training, behavioral scientists have found that solving problems need not be a hit-or-miss, trial-and-error process. The approach to problem solving, especially in a group context, can be systematic, straightforward, and far-reaching.

Let us assume that we are going to have a work conference attended by 200 persons. (For design purposes, the total number of conferees is not particularly relevant, except from a facility and arrangement standpoint. We could have 500 in attendance or as few as 30; the design should remain essentially the same.) We have arranged the 200 persons into 20 ten-person groups. Incidently, we have arranged many other aspects ahead of time as well, such as the training of 20 group discussion leaders. This and other aspects of planning will be covered in the text section. The 20 groups should remain intact throughout the conference. Except for the possibility of a keynote speaker and, in certain instances, a closing speech, the entire time should be spent in either the small discussion groups or in general session where the groups give reports of their work. Let us further assume that now the keynote address has been given, and we are ready for work. The basic format of the conference, at this point, should follow the eight steps of the problem-solving process. All groups are involved in the same step at the same time, even though two-three steps may be covered in any one time block. Let us consider each of these eight steps. Notice that the same process of problem solving may be used regardless of the content of the problems themselves; that is, the problems for discussion may be in the area of faculty and/or student desegregation in public schools, organizational restructuring due to a technological change, community relations as a function of an urban renewal project, etc.

Steps in Problem Solving

Seven of the eight steps should be sequential while the eighth one should operate concurrently throughout the process.

Step 1—Defining the problem: Usually this step begins with asking the groups to identify as many problems or problem areas as they can. In other words, a problem census is taken. Typically, most groups identify many of the same problem areas, so each group is asked to select only one problem for their work. In implementing this first step, three points are stressed: (a) the group should work to obtain clarity and understanding of the problem. Groups usually begin a problem-solving task with the assumption that everyone knows what the problem is and, consequently, there is no clear understanding nor a common definition of the problem. Moreover, when groups attempt to define a problem, or facets thereof, they tend to state the problem in such a way that a solution is implied—or possibly explicitly declared—in the statement. When problems are stated in solution form, this tends to block or inhibit creativity that might occur when a variety of alternative solutions can be suggested. (b) In stating their problem for work, the group should be as specific as possible. For example, if the conference concerns faculty desegregation in public schools, a statement of a problem as "widespread prejudice" is too broad. When the groups begin working on solutions, it is difficult to think of feasible action steps which members themselves can take when they return home or back to their jobs to such a problem. (c) As a last phase of this step, the group should reach agreement that the problem being defined is really the problem. The remaining steps in the process depend on this agreement, especially the solution steps. This particular step may take one session of an hour or so, or it could take two work sessions with a general or plenary session in between. The first session would be a problem census phase with the second period being that of selecting and refining one specific problem. During this general session, several or all of the groups might give a listing of the problems they identified. Thus, this information would be shared with all conferees.

Step 2—Gathering information: This step involves the groups' providing incidents or cases which exemplify the problem. The groups should also discuss certain issues and concerns which appear to be related to the problem. This step helps the conferees to gain a deeper understanding of the problem which, in turn, should assist them in becoming more realistic in their comprehension as well as in their providing solutions.

Step 3—Diagnosing and analyzing the causes: This step may involve the group's thinking of and discussing certain factors which seem to be causing the problem, or the step may be more systematic by not only diagnosing the problem, but analyzing it within a theoretical framework concerned with the dynamics of change. To be more specific, when we have a problem, we usually can establish a goal for alleviating it, an objective for change. We want to *change* the situation so that the problem either diminishes or no longer exists. A noted behavioral scientist of the 1930's and '40's, Kurt Lewin, developed a model for analyzing a problem situation. According to Lewin, no problem situation is static. There are dynamic "forces" that impinge on the situation constantly. Some of these forces drive the problem situation in the direction of change (a problem smoker being afraid of lung cancer—fear being a driving force), and other forces restrain the situation or resist change (the problem smoker relieves his tension by smoking). Thus, by conducting a Force Field Analysis, as Lewin called it, on a problem, i.e., identifying a variety of driving and restraining forces, a group can not only diagnose causes of a problem, but, also, consider an objective for change and how one might bring about this change.

An additional step, at this point, is to include the process of selecting a certain force, or group of forces, for change. In other words, the groups should spend some time on deciding which force(s) to increase or decrease to bring about change or movement toward a stated objective. To summarize, Step 3 should include (a) a statement of a goal or objective for change, (b) each group's conducting a Force Field Analysis, and possibly, (c) selecting certain forces for modification.

Step 4—Proposing solutions: The main objective of this step is for the groups to think of as many alternative solutions for handling the problem as they can. We are not interested in the one best solution at this point: we want a large variety from which we can later make some choices. Implementing this step may take the form of either the groups' conducting a "brainstorming" session or simply taking the time to list determinedly and creatively as many alternative solutions as they can. Often brainstorming as a method can be fun as well as creative. For this to happen, at least two important rules for conducting a brainstorming session should be followed closely. The first rule is that a limited amount of time should be alloted; probably five minutes at the most. Secondly, during the brainstorming no evaluative comments should be made by anyone. The group members should feel completely free to suggest *any* solution, regardless of how silly or unrealistic it may sound. One member of each group should serve as a recorder during the brainstorming.

Step 5—Discussing solutions: Usually this step can follow Step 4 immediately, i.e., within the same meeting period. Now the groups should be evaluative regarding the alternative solutions. Each alternative should be evaluated in terms of the advantages and disadvantages involved. Next, the alternative solutions should be ranked from best to poorest.

Step 6—Deciding on a solution: When deciding on a solution, or a series of solutions, the groups should follow certain criteria. First, their solution(s) should meet a stringent test of feasibility, that is, it should be examined carefully with respect to its potential for success. Secondly, the solution should be one that the members themselves can implement, or at least be involved in implementing. Typically, the group's solution(s) should not be one for the "board to do" or for a "committee to be formed to study the problem further."

Step 7—Planning action steps: Finally, the groups should spend time planning, in considerable detail, definite steps for implementing the solution(s). Involved in these plans should be specific steps which the group members themselves can take. It should be stressed that this planning should be quite specific. For example, in a recent conference with school teachers, one group's solution to their particular problem was to have a "called" faculty meeting upon their return home and to inform their fellow teachers about the nature of the conference they were presently attending. A question the coordinator raised at this point was, "Who is going to be responsible for seeing the principal about arranging this faculty meeting?" This incident may seem rather picky or finicky, but often the best of intentions are never fulfilled. Steps 5, 6, and 7 are usually taken in one session.

Step 8—Evaluating the groups' work: Although this action is listed as Step 8, it should not be a sequential one. Step 8 should be implemented throughout the problem-solving process. This step involves the group members' expressing their feelings about the way they as a group are functioning, i.e., periodically discussing their opinions about the process of how they are working with one another. At the same time, they should plan ways in which they can improve their working relationships. Groups should be reminded of this Step throughout the conference.

TABLE 1

Steps in Problem-Solving

1. Defining the problem
    a. Obtaining clarity and understanding
    b. Being as specific as possible
    c. Reaching agreement that the problem being defined is really the problem

2. Gathering information
    a. Providing incidents or cases that exemplify the problem
    b. Discussing issues and concerns that are related to the problem

3. Diagnosing and analyzing the causes
    a. Stating goal or objective for change
    b. Performing a force field analysis
    c. Selecting force(s) for modification

4. Proposing solutions
    a. "Brainstorming"
    b. Making a list of as many alternative solutions as possible

5. Discussing solutions
    a. Evaluating the merits of each alternative solution
    b. Ranking alternative solutions from best to poorest

6. Deciding on a solution or a series of solutions
    a. Choosing a solution which seems feasible, i.e., has potential for success
    b. Choosing a solution which *we* can actually implement, not someone else

7. Planning action steps
    a. Listing detailed steps for implementing solution(s)
    b. Planning specific steps that we as individuals can take

*8. Evaluating our way of working with one another during the problem-solving process
    a. Expressing our feelings and opinions about the way we are working (or will work) together
    b. Planning ways in which we can improve our working relationships

* Although Steps 1-7 are sequential, Step 8 should be implemented concurrently throughout the process.

In summary, the process of the conference should be one of shifting from a general session to small group meetings, back to general session for group reports, summaries, and inputs for next steps, and then back to small groups again. Although the format of following the steps in problem solving along with the group reports in general sessions is fairly basic, variations can be planned quite easily. For example, including training as a part of the conference is often very useful. Some training could be included by planning an exercise on interpersonal communication, for instance, which would come fairly early in the conference. Also, an occasional theoretical or conceptual input in the form of a brief lecture, seminar, or dialogue could be a beneficial addition. Another variation might be a reorganization of the conferees. For example, during the first half of the conference, groups may be organized heterogeneously for the problem-solving process, and then reorganized more homogeneously, like local, geographical groupings, or similar job responsibilities, etc. The problem-solving process could then be conducted again, this time according to problems of a more localized nature. A sample schedule for a two-day (beginning on a Monday evening and concluding with lunch on Wednesday) conference on problem solving is presented in Table 2.

TABLE 2

A Sample Schedule of a Two-Day Conference on Problem Solving

MONDAY

6:00-7:30 p.m.—Dinner

7:30-8:00 p.m.—Keynote Address

8:00-8:15 p.m.—Format/Plan for Conference and Instructions to Small Groups by Conference Coordinator

TUESDAY

7:30-8:30 a.m.—Breakfast

8:30-9:00 a.m.—General Session: (1) Reports from some of the groups regarding last night's work. (2) Brief lecture on how to implement Steps 3 and 8.

9:00-10:00 a.m.—Group Meeting—Work on Step 3

10:00-10:30 a.m.—Coffee

10:30-11:00 a.m.—General Session: (1) Reports from some of the groups regarding their work on Step 3. (2) Instructions for implementing Steps 4, 5, and 6.

11:00-12:00 noon—Group Meetings—Work on Steps 4, 5, and 6

12:00-1:00 p.m.—Lunch

1:00-1:45 p.m.—General Session: (1) Several groups present their solutions. (2) Instructions for implementing Step 7.

1:45-3:00 p.m.—Group Meetings—Work on Step 7

3:00-3:30 p.m.—General Session: (1) Coke and Coffee. (2) Several groups present their plans for action steps.

3:30-6:00 p.m.—Free Time

6:00-7:15 p.m.—Dinner

7:15-7:30 p.m.—General Session: (1) Change groupings—reorganized according to local geographical patterns. (2) Instructions for implementing Steps 1, 2, and 3 of the Problem-Solving Process.

7:30-9:00 p.m.—Group Meetings—Work on Steps 1, 2, and 3

WEDNESDAY

7:30-8:30 a.m.—Breakfast

8:30-9:00 a.m.—General Session: (1) Review of last evening's work. (2) Instructions for work on Steps 4, 5, and 6.

9:00-10:00 a.m.—Group Meetings—Work on Steps 4, 5, and 6

10:00-10:30 a.m.—Coffee

10:30-11:00 a.m.—General Session: (1) Group reports regarding work on Steps 4-6. (2) Instructions for work on Step 7.

11:00-12:00 Noon—Group Meetings—Work on Step 7

12:00-12:15 p.m.—General Session—Review of groups' work on Step 7

12:15-1:00 p.m.—Lunch

1:00-1:15 p.m.—Summary of Conference by Coordinator

1:15-1:45 p.m.—Closing Address

1:45-1:50 p.m.—Closing Remarks and Adjournment

NOTE: It should be pointed out that all of the General Sessions are held in conjunction with a meal or a coffee break. Thus, the two activities can be held in the same room with conferees seated at tables.

Establishing a Climate for Work: Plans and Activities Before the Conference

As mentioned earlier, establishing a conducive climate for work and a smooth running conference requires some systematic endeavor beforehand. In the short time period of such a conference, maximum effort must be exerted in this area if any changes are to occur. The areas of concern in developing and maintaining an appropriate climate are as follows: (1) the training of group discussion leaders two-three days immediately preceding the conference; (2) obtaining the services of highly qualified consultants to conduct the leadership training and later serve as coordinators for the conference; (3) arranging for adequate facilities for the training period with the group discussion leaders as well as for the conference itself; (4) providing administrative and clerical staff for both phases—the training phase and during the conference; and (5) planning for an adequate budget to ensure maximum flexibility for the leadership training and the conference functions. Each of the five dimensions listed contributes to the development of an atmosphere which is conducive for individual growth as well as skill development in problem solving. To ensure that these five dimensions of concern are managed properly, three different roles or areas of responsibilities are required. There should be the consultant role whose primary responsibilities are that of training the group discussion leaders, helping to plan the conference, and coordinating the conference. Some person or persons to assume the administrative responsibilities as a second role is a must. The third role, and probably the most important one, is that of group discussion leader.

The five dimensions along with the three roles will be discussed in detail.

The training of group discussion leaders, composed of a limited number from the client system forms the linkage between the two aspects of an effective conference—the problem-solving process and establishing a conducive climate for work. There are many skills necessary for an effective discussion leader. First of all, a discussion leader is seen as an individual who has developed skills and techniques which enable all individuals in his group to feel free enough to express themselves openly on the issue or problem concerning the conference. These skills include the areas of interpersonal communication, more awareness of the impact of oneself on others, and insight into the many roles and role barriers which may be present in their group. A second important aspect of skill development is in problem-solving techniques. Development of skills in both areas involves specialized training since these skills deal with "self-development" insights as well as substantive knowledge. One of the major reasons why there is no commitment to change at many work conferences is because both of these areas are not covered. For a detailed description of a design for training group discussion leaders in a two-three day period, see a recent article by Ellis and Burke.[1]

Qualified consultants are needed in three phases of the problem-solving work conference. These areas are (a) training leaders for group discussion and problem-solving skills, (b) preplanning and designing the conference, and (c) serving as the conference coordinator(s) as well as consultant(s) to the newly trained leaders. Preplanning should actively involve the consultants, trained leaders, and conference administrators. Besides enabling the consultants to obtain a necessary feel for the local situation, it also enables them to diagnose the issues in relationship to that particular group of conferees. For example, the problem of desegregation can be defined as one or a multitude of problems. Within this context the issues are different within each local area concerned with this problem. These important differences must be taken into account in designing the problem-solving conference. At least one day should be allowed for the trainers to consult with the conference administrators or "client" and help to design the conference.

Adequate facilities are needed for the training of discussion leaders as well as for the conference. During the training period one large room and four small rooms are desirable. This number assumes that the number of discussion leaders to be trained does not exceed thirty-two. This allows small group (about 8 members in each) as well as large group exercises to be used in the training. If possible, arrangements and facilities should be made for this group to eat their meals together. The added advantage of having the group leaders stay in (hotel or motel) or near the place of training during this period increases the effectiveness of the training.

With respect to the facilities for the conference, consider-

---

[1] Ellis, Betty R. and Burke, W. W. A Design for Training Discussion Leaders. See page 169.

able space is needed. A large room, assuming the number of participants is between 200-600, is needed to conduct the formal and general sessions of the work conference, as well as chairs and tables for the conferees. In addition, one small room is needed for each discussion group. If the location is a hotel or motel, bedrooms can be used. Two microphones are needed—one standing microphone for general sessions and one roving microphone for work sessions conducted in a large group setting. One additional fairly large room is needed for office equipment, supplies, and meeting room for the consultants, conference administrators, and discussion leaders. This additional room, which should be centrally located, can also serve as the dissemination point for printed materials for the conferees.

Adequate staff for administrative responsibilities is needed with authority to accomplish the groundwork necessary before the conference. The administrative staff in the period of time preceding the conference has a myriad of tasks. These tasks center around selecting and informing the discussion leaders and participants of the conference, follow-up contact to ensure the presence of both groups, making arrangements for the facilities, all publicity, ordering supplies and equipment and follow through on these items until delivered. At the beginning of the conference, name tags need to be ready and registration handled as efficiently as possible. Secretarial help is needed throughout the training period and during the conference. During the conference two trained secretaries are needed to type dittoes, operate ditto machine, and possibly, transcribe tape recordings as well as handle registration and the miscellaneous details surrounding a work conference. It is a must that the individuals assigned by the client system to aid in the operation of the conference have the authority to make decisions in relationship to facilities and supplies.

The consultants need to have considerable responsibility for the design of the conference. As each part of the design is planned to help the conferees solve problems, the consultants need flexibility in control or change of the conference design to ensure overall success.

Large enough budget items are needed for the operating of a conference to ensure maximum feedback to the participants. Supplies in the form of kits are needed for each discussion leader for use in their small group. Each kit should include newsprint, two magic markers, masking tape, 10-15 ditto masters, and possibly tape for recording the sessions. The training sessions and the large general sessions of the conference also need a large supply of the items listed above. The office supplies needed are one typewriter, two ditto machines and fluid, paper at least equal to 15-20 sheets per participant, and several tape recorders.

An important part of the conference design is that of providing information concerning the work of each problem-solving group to all other groups. This is accomplished in at least two ways. One is that several groups report their work, via newsprint and oral summaries, at each general session. Another way is through duplication. During certain small group work sessions, e.g., Steps 1, sometimes 3, 6, and 7 of the Problem-Solving Process, the group recorder prints on a ditto master a summary of the group's work for that session. Later these dittoes are duplicated and distributed to all of the conferees. Providing this information not only shares the benefit of good ideas, but it also acts as a motivating force for small group work.

SUMMARY

The success of most any conference usually depends on two key factors: (1) the extent to which conferees participate or become personally involved in the conference process, and (2) whether or not anything is *accomplished* at the conference or groundwork is laid for action following the conference. Of course, there are many different kinds of conferences. Some are for the purpose of information dissemination only, while others involve professional business. If one desires a conference which aims for exchange of information, the discussing and working on problems, as well as action of one kind or the other, then there are effective ways of planning and conducting one. The type of conference outlined in this paper does not allow for (a) a parade of speakers, (b) uninvolvement on the part of the conferees, nor (c) a two to three day period of extended socializing and/or politicking. While these three elements may indeed be a part of the conference (item (c) is inevitable), systematic work on real problems can be conducted.

Since the 1940's, conferences have expanded in number and complexity. The conference today is an integral part of many persons' lives, especially professionals. The conference will continue to be needed in the future and, in all likelihood, it will continue to expand. Computers and television will become integral parts of tomorrow's conference. Along with the new "hardware," however, we must continue to improve our technology in the utilization of *human* resources. The design presented in this paper is an attempt in this direction.

What Makes a Convention Tick?

RICHARD BECKHARD

The convention is a high point in the annual activities of an organization. Frequently, weeks and months of effort go into the planning. Large sums of money are spent by the organization and by the members attending the convention. In addition to the entire budget of a convention which, for a large one, can run from $20,000 to several hundred thousand dollars, the travel expenses of 1000 delegates to a national meeting can be conservatively estimated at $200,000. Every meeting planner must face the question: Is there a satisfactory return? How can we increase the return?

Most conventions have one or more of the following stated purposes:

1. To conduct the organization's business
2. To give new information or policies to delegates
3. To exchange experiences and ideas
4. To allow delegates to make contacts
5. To meet together socially with colleagues.

Anyone who has ever planned a large meeting is well aware of the difficulties of accomplishing these several objectives at any one convention. The requirements of each objective are quite different and demand different treatment. The problem becomes more acute as the attendance at conventions

Reprinted by special permission of the JOURNAL OF THE AMERICAN TRADE ASSOCIATION EXECUTIVES (now the JOURNAL OF THE AMERICAN SOCIETY OF ASSOCIATION EXECUTIVES) and of the author.

increases. Independent surveys have shown that large numbers of convention-goers are becoming increasingly less satisfied with the typical annual convention. Some of the reasons
they give are these: "You never get to see anybody anymore—
just mill around with a mob." "Too much partying. I'd rather
stay home with my friends if I want a party." "Nothing new
or different happens. It's the same thing every year."

Because of the number of meetings involved in management operations today, the convention finds itself competing
with a number of other meetings which every executive must
attend. The convention-goer no longer looks forward to the
annual convention as his "big trip" of the year.

There are a number of things that a meeting planner can
do to deal with these facts. We know a lot more about what
makes meetings tick today than we did a few years ago. Social
scientists have developed a good deal of information on member participation and the systematic appraisal of meetings.

A first step is to identify the factors that impede the effectiveness of meetings. Here are 10 common reasons why some
meetings do not pay off:

1. The objectives of planners are unrealistic or unattain-
   able.
2. The audience does not agree with or understand the
   objectives.
3. The audience is not interested in the material presented.
4. The audience does not feel any responsibility or concern
   about the success of the meeting—it is not their worry.
5. The material is poorly presented.
6. The speakers are inadequately prepared.
7. The speakers talk down to the audience.
8. The physical facilities are poor—the audience cannot
   see or hear.
9. The audience would rather be somewhere else or doing
   something else, but their opinions have not been asked.
10. The audience expresses resistance or hostility toward
    platform participants.

Today's businessman wants to take home some ideas he
can use—ideas that will pay off in some way. Otherwise, he
considers his attendance at a meeting a waste of time. Meeting planners must take this fact into account throughout the
planning.

There are a few basic principles of planning a meeting that must be observed if it is to satisfy both the planners and the audience:

1. The planners must have a clearly defined objective for the total meeting and for each session. These objectives must be realistic and attainable.

2. The planners should know their audience's interests and what audience members expect to receive from the meeting. These interests and expectations must be related to the objectives.

3. Planners should insure that audience members feel that the meeting is concerned with their problems and is of importance to them. Audience members should participate in the planning, wherever possible.

4. Presentation methods for each item of subject matter should be devised in terms of both the material to be presented and the situation in which it will be presented.

5. Planners should test the effectiveness of the communication at the meeting and again after the meeting in order to improve subsequent meetings.

6. Systematic follow-up procedures should be devised as part of the planning in order to assure adequate "take-home pay" for the delegates.

Defining and Clarifying the Objectives

Most meeting planners would be insulted if one were to question how clear were the objectives of a meeting. Yet there is a substantial body of evidence to indicate that many meetings fail because they lack clear objectives. One way of testing the objectives and clarifying them in the early planning is to state them in terms of "hoped-for outcomes" for delegates. What do you want the delegate to take away with him—from the entire meeting, and from each session? One convention-planning group has created a "Mr. Jones," the typical delegate, and every bit of planning is tested in terms of his reactions. The executives who have been 'playing" Mr. Jones in planning-committee meetings have come to think of him as an actual member of the committee. This testing of objectives and developing of an actual statement of objectives create a yardstick against which all program planning can be measured.

Determining the Audience's Needs and Expectations

Frequently, when Mr. Jones is asked what he wants or is expecting, we find considerable disagreement among planners about what they think he *does* want; or the planners may be sure they know what he wants and discover at a meeting that he did not want that at all.

We have had a number of experiences in working in situations where the national office of an association or the management of an industry has told us what the problems of the delegates were. However, interviews with delegates, prior to the meeting, have frequently shown delegates' perceptions of their problems to be quite different from those of the planners. Such a situation implies the need for developing some systematic method for obtaining from delegates themselves their ideas about what they consider key problems and what they want discussed. The mere procedure of asking for this information accomplishes several things:

1. It forces the individual delegate to think about the meeting before he goes to it.
2. It causes the individual delegate to feel important.
3. It increases the individual delegate's interest in the meeting because he has participated in planning part of it. (It may be curiosity alone to learn whether his problem will actually be discussed that prompts him to participate in the planning.)
4. It furnishes the planners with valuable information for agenda preparation.
5. It helps the planners to select priorities and allot time on the basis of the degree of interest in any given subject.

Too many meetings are planned on the basis of hunches about delegates' interests. It is relatively simple today to assemble the facts which assure sounder and more accurate planning.

Involving Audience Members and Securing Participation

All of us are concerned with the problem of eliciting audience participation. Toward this end, a number of techniques have been developed. In some instances, they are used without thought about their relationship to the subject matter and the audience attitudes, with the result that the meeting "lays an egg." Such techniques are useful only if they are practical in the particular situation.

The involvement of audience members can start prior to the meeting itself by the use of premeeting information and data-collection devices. If every delegate attending a meeting feels that it is truly concerned with his problems and that, as a concomitant circumstance, he has a stake in the meeting itself, the meeting cannot but be more active and meaningful to all.

At the meeting itself, opportunities should be created for educing reactions to presentation from audience members. It is not always possible to have discussion groups in large conventions, but there are a number of devices that can be used to increase participation and the feeling of involvement. Questions from the floor provide some participation, but also create problems of time in a large meeting. It is also true that a number of people who might have questions do not ask them lest they take up other people's time. One device that circumvents this difficulty and creates a genuine feeling of participation is the question pad. If delegates are furnished pads on which they can write questions *as they occur to them*, and if procedures are built in for handling these questions, every audience member feels that he has the opportunity for participation—whether or not he takes advantage of it. In certain situations the Phillips 66 or buzz-group technique is effective: Units of six to eight persons turn their chairs into a circle and discuss a subject which they then report to the entire meeting. There are a number of similar techniques which can be used to increase the actual involvement.

Devising Meeting Methods

Most meeting planners and those who attend meetings agree that "we should have fewer speeches." Yet meeting after meeting still schedules a series of speeches! One reason for this is that many meeting planners feel insecure in trying out other methods of presentation. Another reason is that it is difficult to determine what method to use if you do not use a speech.

All platform presentations may be placed in one of the following categories:

1. Unassisted speech
2. Speech with audiovisual aids
3. Demonstration
4. Situation presentation
5. Dramatic action presentation
6. Panel-symposium forum

Each of these methods has its own characteristics, and there is a more or less systematic way of determining which of them meets the situation best. Thus, in summary:

If the subject matter is the presentation of a new organization plan, a visual exhibit or chart presentation would logically be called for. On the other hand, if the subject matter is on leadership techniques, the chart presentation would be inappropriate and an unassisted speech would have little effect. The audience needs to see a situation of good leadership techniques in action. Here, a situation presentation is needed. By testing each element of subject matter in terms of its own characteristics and the situation in which it will be presented (audience attitudes, interest in subject, and so on), the planner has a set of real criteria for determining presentation method.

Appraising the Effectiveness of the Convention

There are a number of methods of establishing measures of the feelings of satisfaction, kinds of interest, and attitudes of an audience. Such measures can provide meeting planners with specific ideas for improving subsequent meetings. One of the simplest methods is an end-of-the-meeting reaction sheet. This can be a one-page questionnaire in which the respondent is asked what he liked most and liked least and why. He can also be asked for suggestions for subsequent meetings.

A more accurate measure can be obtained by giving to a sample of the group or to the entire group a questionnaire or brief interview immediately before the convention and again immediately after it. Questions such as "What are the three major problems you hope will be discussed?" in a premeeting questionnaire become more meaningful when you ask the same person "What problems did you bring to the meeting that were not dealt with to your satisfaction?" as a postmeeting question. Interviews of a small, selected sample provide even more accurate information, but such interviews should be conducted only by trained interviewers who should not be identified with the leadership of the organization.

A questionnaire or interview sheet sent to delegates a few weeks after a convention, asking them what items of the program stand out in their memories and what items of the program have been most useful in their back-home jobs, will provide the planner with a good start on the planning of his next meeting. All of these measurement techniques have one other beneficial effect: they strengthen the feeling on the part of the delegate that the meeting is for him and what he says is important.

Planning the Follow-Up

One of the most important ground rules for a meeting whose purpose is to create some change is to plan the followup while you plan the meeting. Too many meetings are thought of as isolated activities rather than as media by which the organization is given a boost. If you want a delegate to do something about what he receives from a meeting, you have to (a) invite him to think about this before he arrives at the meeting, (b) provide help to him during the meeting, and (c) provide continuing assistance in the form of information, conference reports, or new facts after the meeting. Most of us tend to forget about the meeting after we get back home to our jobs. A brief and usable report, a mimeographed copy of an effective speech, a reprint of some charts, or a questionnaire asking opinions of the meeting—all these serve to refresh the delegate's memory about the meeting and stimulate him to do something about it back home.

Although there is no quick panacea that will guarantee that every meeting will be a gigantic success, the observance of these basic planning principles places the odds in favor of a successful result. Ask yourself these questions:

1. Is the objective of the whole meeting and of each session clear? realistic? attainable?

2. Do I *know* the audience? their expectations of the meetings? their problems? Have I taken these problems into account?

3. Will the audience members feel that this is their meeting? Will they have a stake in it?

4. Have I developed the presentation methods from the point of view of both the material to be presented and the situation in which it will be presented?

5. Have I planned any appraisal devices for improving subsequent meetings?

6. What kind of follow-up planning is needed to make the meeting most useful to the delegates?

If you have the answers to these questions, the chances are your convention will tick and click.

BIBLIOGRAPHY

1. Beckhard, Richard, and Beckhard, Alethea T., "Improving Large Meetings." *Adult Leadership* 1: No. 7; December 1952.

2. Edlund, Roscoe C. "They Tell You They Love Your Meetings, But Are You Sure They Mean It?" *Sales Meetings:* 28-33; January 1953.

3. Richard Beckhard Associates. *Planning and Staging Meetings and Conventions.* Chicago: Dartnell Corp., 1952.

4. "Your Business Meeting: Boon or Bore?" *Modern Industry* 24: 58-60; August 15, 1952.

Planning an
International Conference

LELAND P. BRADFORD

Organization and structure should follow func-
tion. Yet all too frequently in the planning and conducting of
conferences, organization and structure work against conference purpose, particularly if that purpose is to stimulate
communication and joint consideration of issues and problems. Too many speeches are scheduled; opportunities for
discussion are too infrequent or too brief; and parts of the
program are unrelated to other parts. There is little sense of
"flow" or progression.

Frequently, conference planners are plagued by conference
facilities that do not lend themselves to effective confer-
ring. Seats are fixed in conventional auditorium style, or conference tables are long and narrow. Far from facilitating,
facilities actually become obstacles to face-to-face discussion and, hence, to any real communication

Ineffective conference procedures and inadequate facilities
work against success in domestic conferences. They are
double barriers in international conferences, where differences in language, philosophy, and culture are themselves
barriers to communication.

This paper is a description of one effort to develop an
effective conference organization and to adapt available
conference facilities so that genuine communication, joint
identification of problems, and discussions leading toward
action solutions could occur. The occasion was an inter-

national conference on adult education.[1] Adult educators
from many countries were invited to attend, along with
educators from other areas of specialization so that closer
relationships could develop among adult educators and other
professional educators in and among the countries represented.

The small planning committee, because of limited time and
finances, was from the United States alone. The committee
members were under no illusions that they knew the solutions to problems in adult education in various parts of the
world, or indeed that they were even very certain what these
problems might be. The committee did believe that joint
efforts to determine common problems might create among
participants a desire to continue to communicate with one
another and, at the same time, might stimulate further
problem solving at local and regional levels. It was assumed
that such continued communication would significantly
benefit adult education in various places throughout the
world.

The basic purposes of the Conference, therefore, were
these: to stimulate communication among educators, to
identify common problems, to share solutions being tried
throughout the world, and to work out ways of continuing to
relate to one another. Conference procedures were needed
to create opportunities for the participants to become
acquainted, to facilitate their joint analysis of problems in
adult education, and to encourage collaborative work toward
the solution of such problems.

Physical Arrangements

The facilities available consisted of one very large conference
room with a high stage at one end. (As other conferences
were being held simultaneously in the building, every other
room was in use.) Normally, this conference room was used
as an auditorium. The rows of seats, however, could be removed and, in this instance, had been removed. To compli-
cate this somewhat discouraging physical setting, the auditorium was set up with long, narrow tables, left from the
preceding meeting. There was no time between the end of
the previous meeting and the beginning of the present Con-

---

[1] The International Conference on Adult Education, sponsored jointly by the
National Education Association of the United States and the World Confederation
of Organizations of the Teaching Profession, Washington, D. C., July 22-29, 1959.

ference to do any rearranging. The conference room, therefore, looked like Figure 1:

FIGURE 1

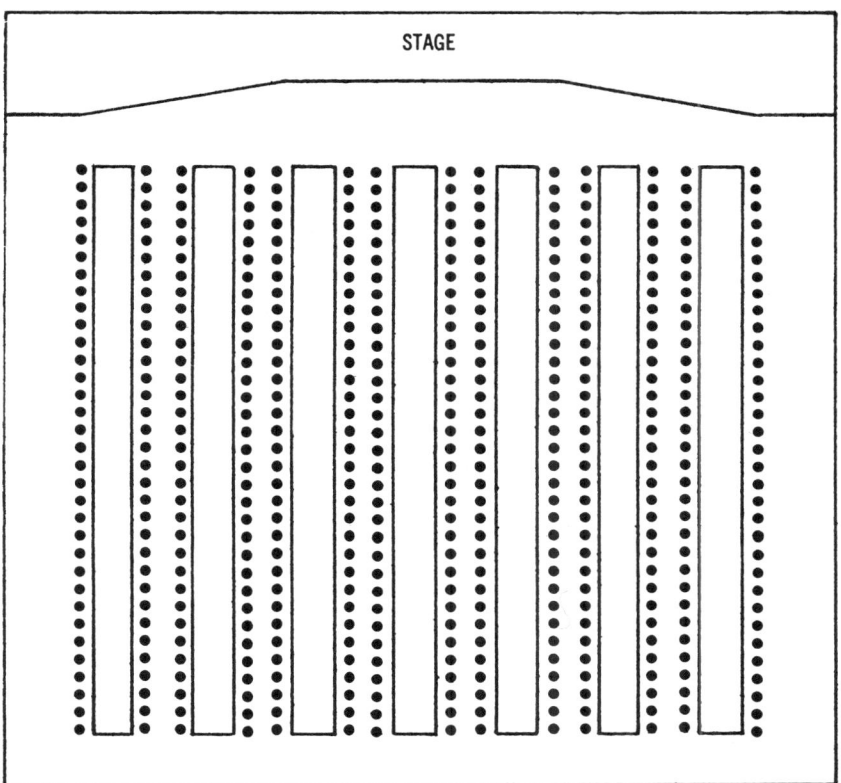

The long, narrow tables, stretching almost the length of the
auditorium, seated several hundred persons. Since about a
hundred participants were expected to attend, obviously only
a fraction of the table space would be occupied. The planning
staff faced the problem of fostering interpersonal communication within these physical limitations.

As the planners worked things out, the physical situation,
which looked so discouraging, actually lent itself to small-
group discussion. By removing every fourth and fifth chair
from each side of each table, small face-to-face groups of
six persons each were formed. The narrowness of the tables

thus became an advantage rather than a handicap. The conference room now looked like Figure 2:

FIGURE 2

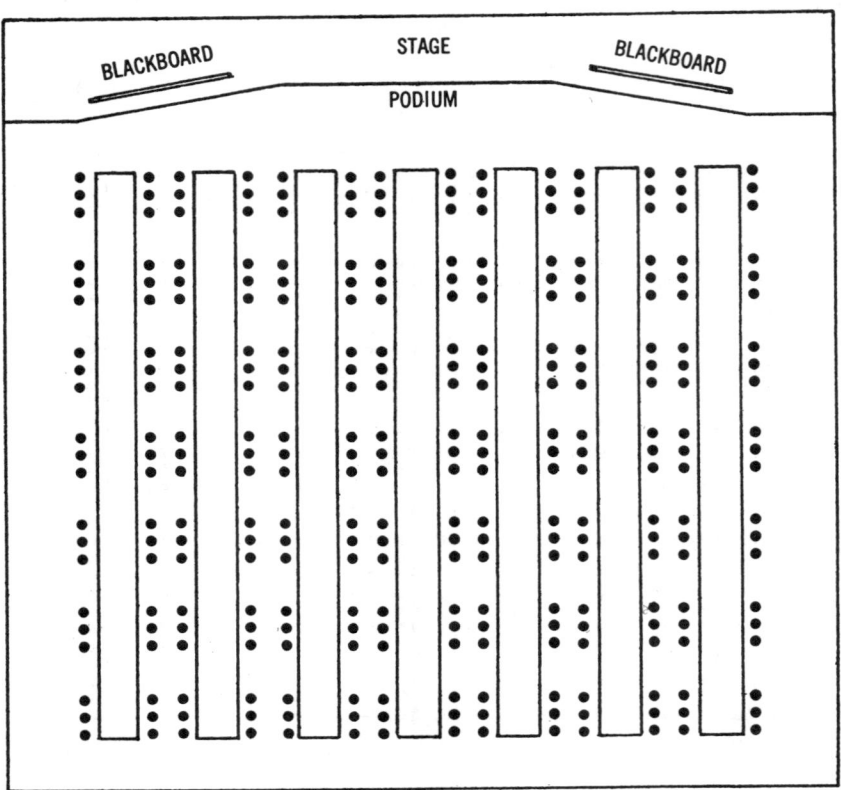

Program Design

The Conference program began with the customary, but brief, welcomes, a statement of its basic purpose and hoped-for consequences, and a reference to plans for continued communication that might emerge from it.

On the stage were two large blackboards, one on each side of a podium. One board carried a list of a few problem areas in adult education that, in the judgment of the planners, might be relevant for adult educators in various lands. The other board was blank.

The director of the Conference described the plans and asked the naturally formed groups of six at the tables to introduce themselves to one another and to consider the problems listed on the blackboard in terms of possible modifications or deletions and to consider additional problems to be listed on the blank blackboard.

Only a few revisions or additions were made, but they were important. The rush of conversation and comments heard later gave evidence that this first session helped to start a process of communication and to remove much of the initial stiffness. With random seating encouraged, the session also served to discharge tendencies for homogeneous cultural groupings to form.

The second session, held under identical conditions, encouraged further communication and group effort toward problem definition and planning. Each member of a panel, representative of the major geographical areas of the world, was asked to react to the revised problems now listed on the board by illustrating them out of experience in his own country. This procedure seemed to serve the threefold purpose of sharing experiences, clarifying common concerns, and giving visibility to those sections of the world that were represented. It demonstrated not only differences but also some basic similarities in goals and concerns.

By the morning of the second day, time had been found to remove the tables from the auditorium. In their place, five large circles of chairs (approximately 18 in each circle) had been set up. (See Figure 3.) The five circles, sufficiently distant from one another so that there was little sound interference, were arranged in the shape of a horseshoe. At the opening, a table with five chairs (for a panel representing the five groups) was placed at an angle, with a chair and smaller table for an interrogator. Between the two tables were two large blackboards.

Each of the five groups was assigned a skilled discussion leader whose job was to help the group go further in exploring the problems brought out the previous day in terms of issues represented and suggestions for action. The groups were heterogeneously formed as to language, area represented, and professional interests. Each group decided what language it would use, and in a few groups Spanish or French was spoken for much of the time.

Periodically during the day, group action would be stopped,

and representatives of the groups, selected by each group, would take seats at the panel table. With help from the

FIGURE 3

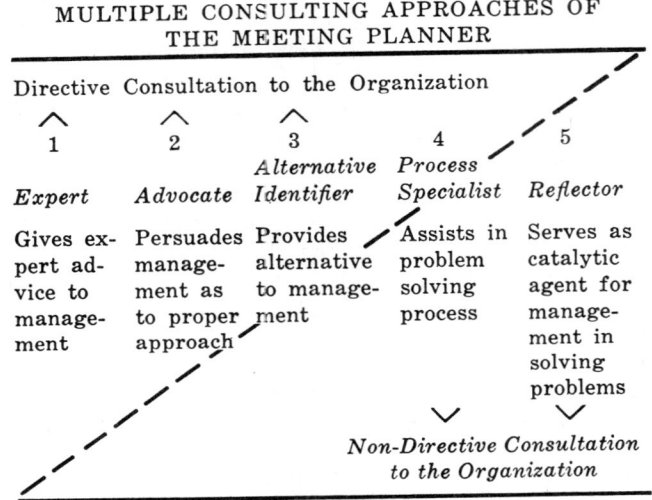

MULTIPLE CONSULTING APPROACHES OF
THE MEETING PLANNER

Directive Consultation to the Organization

1	2	3	4	5
		Alternative	*Process*	
Expert	*Advocate*	*Identifier*	*Specialist*	*Reflector*
Gives expert advice to management	Persuades management as to proper approach	Provides alternative to management	Assists in problem solving process	Serves as catalytic agent for management in solving problems

*Non-Directive Consultation
to the Organization*

interrogator, the panel would then bring out issues or suggestions emerging from the discussions at each table. These issues or suggested solutions were listed on the blackboards. As they were discussed by panel members, any member of any of the five groups could go—and numbers did go—to one of the floor microphones to express ideas or suggestions stimulated by the panel discussion.

When issues had been elaborated upon and new questions and issues interjected from the panel or from the floor, panel members would return to their groups for further discussion. Later, panel members would return to the panel table for another total conference session. Sometimes the same group representatives were returned to the panel; sometimes different representatives were named.

The conference planners anticipated that certain values would be gained from this design. With individuals coming from many countries and with the resulting cultural, language, and other differences, suspicion of closed sessions or sessions in which only speeches would be given could be anticipated. The design used meant that each group discussed the same or similar issues in full sight of all the others. Periodic sampling of group progress through the interrogator-panel process made the progress and direction of each group clear to all. It was possible for groups to influence other groups and for individuals to influence other individuals or the conference as a whole. At the same time, participation by every individual was made possible and encouraged through the small-group structure. Decisions about future plans were made openly.

Participation

While no systematic comparison was made, periodic observations were made of this conference and another more formally structured international conference that was being held at the same time in another part of the building. One purpose of the observation was to check the degree of participation in each of the conferences and the extent to which individuals stayed with the conference or came and went. The observations indicated that for the periods observed, participation was wider and holding power greater in the Adult Education Conference than in the more formally structured conference.

This effort suggests that, with careful planning, conference facilities, even when they seem unfavorable, can be fitted to conference purposes and desired consequences when such purposes and consequences are clearly understood.

The Conference as an Intervention in a Community-School Conflict

GILBERT LEVIN and
DAVID D. STEIN

During the New York City school strike of 1968, staff members of a community mental health center and members of a local community group organized a forum in school-community relations. The intention was to channel existing conflicts into areas of long-term benefit to the community the CMHC serves. This report is significant—and may be of interest to those planning conferences in similar situations —because several factors are not typical of applied behavioral science interventions.

First, entry took place at the height of a community conflict situation and in the face of warnings from various parties to the conflict that the most constructive course was to do nothing.

Second, the relationship between a community mental health center and its catchment area differs in important respects from that involved in either the external or internal change agent models, and thus limits action alternatives in such a crisis.

Third, turnout at the forum was strikingly high and quite representative of the community population.

Fourth, the design of the forum itself is of interest since it altered successfully some of the chaotic aspects of the typical public meeting.

The Background

In the fall of 1968, New York City was hit by a long and bitter school strike. During those harrowing two months, when schools opened periodically only to close down again after a day or so, parental concern over the education of their children began to affect and to be affected by the issues that had caused the controversy—decentralization of the school board, community control, and teachers' job security. As the resulting community feeling of helplessness grew, the pressure increased on various community agencies to do something—anything—either to help end the school strike or to aid the children (and their parents) in the interim.

One agency affected by these pressures was a community mental health center (CMHC); as the community cries for action became more insistent, center staff members responded by helping to plan and execute a forum in school-community relations. The intention of the forum was to channel existing conflicts in the direction of long-term benefit to the community. The result was not only an apparently successful program, but also an increased closeness and understanding between the CMHC and the community it serves.

Planning for the forum began within CMHC.[1] The population it serves is ethnically and economically heterogeneous, and is changing from a predominantly blue-collar white to a black and Puerto Rican population of relatively lower socioeconomic status. In the school year preceding the strike, CMHC had built a number of significant consultative relationships with schools in its catchment area. When in 1968 the school opening was delayed and the schools were later closed by the strike, the center felt conflicting pressures from teachers and principals and from parents in the area to act in ways that each group construed to be on its behalf. The mixed character of the population caused significant conflict within role groups as well as between them. For example, Local Group (a grass roots parents' group which CMHC had helped to organize for more than a year) was seriously split. Many members supported and contributed to keeping the schools open in defiance of the United Federation of Teachers (UFT); others favored keeping the schools closed. Some mem-

[1] We gratefully acknowledge the assistance of our colleagues Carl Harm, Robert Treat, and Celia South in the planning and implementation of the Forum. Andrew Weiss provided helpful editorial assistance.

bers of both factions wanted to set up temporary classrooms outside of school buildings; others opposed this action. While these subgroups were formed in part on racial and ethnic lines, it was not exclusively so. Indeed, CMHC was aware of several incidents of conflict and alienation between neighbors who had maintained amicable, even friendly, relationships over a period of years.

Conflicting pressures on the staff to provide services and/ or to take sides caused considerable tension within CMHC in the initial weeks of the dispute. For example, at least three principals approached CMHC staff known to and trusted by them with requests for services in their schools—this during a period when picket lines composed partly of other CMHC clients were up, and attendance at schools was low. Simultaneously, other teachers and parents from these same schools requested space in the CMHC to hold informal classes. At first, CMHC tried to ride out the storm. Most staff members seemed to favor acting on the needs of individual clients, but to refrain from doing so if it seemed that the collective organizational clients of CMHC might not be served in that way. In addition each staff member was in actual or potential conflict with one or more other CMHC staff members whose personal clientele advocated a contradictory behavior from CMHC. As time passed, staff members became increasingly aware that inaction was jeopardizing relationships they had labored to build. In addition, CMHC observed that its passive attitude was shared by virtually every other organized group with a mandate to act. These pressures from both within and without the center eventually forced it to act, despite the indicated prohibitions against doing so.

After some preliminary planning was completed, CMHC invited Local Group to collaborate in sponsoring and implementing an open meeting aimed at managing the conflict. At the suggestion of its president a Local Group planning committee was formed, with membership constituted so as to give most parties in the conflict a voice in planning. While CMHC and Local Group agreed that a full resolution of the various conflicts was dependent on city-wide forces and negotiations at that level, they also felt that it would be possible to design and implement a program aimed at limited but nevertheless significant objectives. These were worked out in several joint planning sessions.

1. People with strong feelings and definite opinions would be able to examine them in a more rational light.
2. In a defused atmosphere, angry people on each side of an issue would have an opportunity to "hear" the opposing point of view.
3. People with legitimate differences of opinion would be able to come to mutually agreed-upon accommodations.
4. Stereotypes would be reduced, and members of particular groups—racial and ethnic, teacher, parent or student, for instance—would be able to discover advantages in working together.
5. The forum format, or variants of it, would be adopted by various groups to resolve continuing and new conflicts which might emerge in their environments.

These objectives were not arrived at until after members of the planning committee confronted each other with some stereotyped notions. Some parents, for instance—assumed that all teachers were in favor of the strike—an assumption obviously untrue, although few teachers who opposed the strike could afford to make public declarations of their position. Charges of anti-Semitism and black militarism were leveled when people disagreed and did not want to confront the substantive issues underlying their differences. However, such stereotypes were more pervasive in the day-to-day contacts among community members than in the joint planning sessions; there they played a minor role, probably because the committee members seemed anxious by that time to do something constructive.

The Design

The Local Group and CMHC decided to invite a large number of people from both the schools and the community to participate. The capacity of the available auditorium necessitated scheduling two consecutive weekday evenings with 125 people invited each night. The invitation list for each evening was made up of 48 parents (from the 16 public schools in an area defined by the Local Group as its community), 32 teachers, eight school principals, 25 students (grades 9 through 12), one to three clergymen, three to four businessmen, one to three district school superintendents, one to two local school board members, and one policeman from the local precinct. Personal contacts insured the attendance of parents and teachers representing different points of view.

The Forum was held at the CMHC. The schedule of events, modeled after a typical residential laboratory exercise, was as follows:

7:30- 8:00	Warm-Up
8:00- 8:15	Welcome and Orientation
8:15	Sheets Containing "Suggested Issues for Discussion" passed out
8:15- 9:05	Platform and Nomination
9:05- 9:30	Speeches (5 minutes each)
9:30- 9:35	Election (Ballots passed out at 9:30)
9:35-10:15	Discussion of Process and Results
10:15-10:30	Follow-up Steps

From 7:30 to 8:00 p.m., each person was greeted and registered. People were assigned to groups to insure a relative balance of role membership (i.e., teacher, parent, student, principal), and those who came in pairs or cliques were separated to facilitate contacts with new people and points of view. Folding chairs were set up in five groups. Pencils, pads and envelopes were placed on a small table in each circle. On entering the auditorium guests received 10 multiple choice questions about demographic and educational matters related to the schools in the area. Each envelope contained the answer to one question; each person was allowed to open one envelope only. In this way, every individual was included in the discussion; people got to know one another and also learned something about the schools. A CMHC staff person was present in each group during the warm-up period as a facilitator only. This procedure eliminated the build-up—common at community meetings as early arrivals await latecomers—of boredom and of alienation caused by clique formation. Each person became involved in the evening's business as soon as he arrived. Group cohesiveness developed during the warm-up period, making it possible for people to handle the evening's major task, which required a cooperative problem-solving set. Since each person could make a specific contribution to his group when he arrived by opening an envelope and giving the group an answer to a question, his sense of inclusion was enhanced.

The second phase of the program started around 8:15, when a member of Local Group and a member of CMHC made brief welcoming remarks. The five groups were then given instructions concerning their task for the next hour. Each group was requested to develop a platform on a series of education-related issues and at the same time to nominate one of its members as a candidate for mayor in a mock election. The issues suggested were construction and physical improvement of schools, curriculum, parental participation in planning and decision-making, conflict and polarization within and between various groups, the disruptive child, and decentralization.

The inclusion of the mock election in the design was suggested by the situation—a gathering of an urban community organization, not one of individuals familiar with the tenets of applied behavioral science. It was felt that the election had the right amount of "local color"—that participants could identify with this device on political, democratic, cultural or subcultural, even "old-fashioned," lines—more readily than they might with a "sophisticated" decision-making situation.

The groups went to work promptly. Only one person, a member of the local school board, declined to participate, explaining to members of the CMHC in the hall that she felt her access to private information about school matters would inhibit her participation in the forum.

By about 9:15 p.m. each group had nominated its candidate for mayor and the campaign began.

The Platforms

The nominees (a total of 10) included parents, teachers, principals, and students which suggests that no particular role bias influenced the groups' choices of representatives.

Most of the campaign speeches stressed the value of a situation in which people with different views get together to talk productively about issues. Students wanted more opportunity to get to know their teachers, and to substitute exciting educational experiences for the drudgery of school. Specific suggestions were that:

- Neighborhood facilities be used as classrooms to alleviate overcrowding.
- Housing construction be curtailed unless new school facilities were included in plans.
- Community residents be employed in paraprofessional and tutorial roles.
- More minority group teachers be hired.
- Textbooks be geared to minority group experiences. Curricula include such neglected areas as "heritage" studies and the history of labor unions.

- Computer instruction be given.
- School programs for children 2 and 3 years old be provided.
- Vocational training programs place non-college-bound students in skilled and respected positions.
- Student influence in school programming and policy be increased.
- An accountability system—more specific than was then the case, yet fair—be instituted for teachers and school administrators.
- Local school boards be elected.
- School facilities be used during free hours for community recreation and social services such as family and legal counseling.

It should be noted that the forum was not designed to include action assignments, but merely to generate major educational concerns. Nevertheless it is unusual for a community group to be so explicit in its demands for better education. Vague and general exhortations are typical, with little real analysis of specifics.

Process in Platform Preparations

The election was then held by individual written ballot. While the votes were being tallied, the CMHC chairman suggested that someone from each group share with the whole group the experience of his particular unit in working together.

Most groups reported feeling overwhelmed by the difficulty of the task and therefore selected those issues which held the greatest meaning for their members. They reported an open, if not always heated, exchange of views between the various camps represented. Pleasurable surprise at being able to see proponents of differing views as people rather than as ogres was reported. While some individuals tended to dominate the discussion at the beginning, no group felt this continued very long.

Candidates were nominated mainly on the basis of verbal skills demonstrated in the group discussions. On a few occasions, students were nominated because "this was about their education."

It was also generally agreed that this type of forum should be repeated or continued, but at individual schools, not at CMHC.

The Election Results

The mock election provided, as suggested above, a sense of participation in the process of the forum. It resulted in feedback which, although fascinating, is insufficient for interpretation. This could be viewed as a failure of the design; it might also be seen as essential to the structure, significant in its absence.

The election also provides a mechanism for sharing "content" data and for gathering data on the strength of in-group identification (group cohesiveness), and in these areas, particularly the latter, more concrete assessments are possible.

Since participants in each group worked together for a significant period, one would expect each group to cast a high proportion of votes for its own candidate, even though he might not be the choice of the total group. Comments about "our man" or "our girl" indicated this was indeed the case. Group solidarity developed quite strongly in most groups, and members preferred to mantain allegiance to their own candidate rather than to cast a vote for someone else, even one whose presentation merited endorsement. Pulling together to accomplish a clearly designated task no doubt facilitated the development of solidarity; group forces operated to achieve consensus on issues, and divergent views had either to be ignored or assimilated into the platform. A rough measure of this variable is presented in Table I.

TABLE I.

First Night

Group	N	Total Votes Received	Votes from Own Group	Proportion of Own Group votes to total possible Own Group votes	Chance expectation of Own Group votes
1	14	10	9	.64	.20
2	16	17	9	.56	.20
3	15	29	10	.67	.20
4	16	16	11	.69	.20
5	14	3	2	.14	.20

Second Night

Group	N	Total Votes Received	Votes from Own Group	Proportion of Own Group votes to total possible Own Group votes	Chance expectation of Own Group votes
1	11	13	11	1.0	.20
2	11	3	3	.27	.20
3	11	17	11	1.0	.20
4	12	13	9	.75	.20
5	11	10	7	.64	.20

In eight of 10 groups, candidates received appreciably more than random endorsement from their own groups. The two contradictory cases (Group 5 on the first night and Group 2 on the second) can probably be accounted for by the relatively desultory campaign speeches of those candidates. Of importance is the field validation of the behavioral science principle of in-group choice. Numerous examples in laboratory settings have demonstrated this phenomenon after the completion of certain group tasks. In this situation, ideological and attitudinal differences, exacerbated by the school strike, did not obliterate the effect of in-group identification. This result tends to support the authors' guarded optimism about working with community groups in conflict.

Conclusions and Future Possibilities

The evaluation of the forum by the CMHC and the Local Group was very positive. They were delighted that people with opposing points of view could work together productively, and were especially pleased with the attitudes and enthusiasms expressed by the many students who attended. Most people left the meeting with increased feelings of respect for one another. Since the forum, the authors have heard of several people, formerly isolated by opposing positions on sensitive issues, who were subsequently able to discuss their differences.

Some reservations about the success of the forum were voiced by members of the joint CMHC-Local Group planning committee. To some the process seemed a little too smooth: some people did not fully warm up to the point of expressing openly and honestly very strong feelings on the issues related to the strike.

In general, however, the hopes and expectations for the forum were met. Some of those who attended immediately began planning to meet again to begin to cope with these major problems. CMHC intends to assist in the development of such programs.

The Aftermath

As a result of the forum, CMHC has been requested by several parent associations for consultation on and help in establishing clearer goals and priorities through similar workshops. Local Group on its own initiative planned another forum to convert the positive feelings engendered by the earlier meeting into positive action. With CMHC assistance Local Group worked out its own design for a community-wide meeting aimed at setting priorities for local educational improvement and creating task forces to begin implementation.

At the meeting in March 1969 three task forces composed jointly of school personnel and community residents were established. These are called the Narcotics Problems of Youth, More Effective Teaching, and Improvement of School-Community Relations.

The Narcotics task force has begun to work on a monitoring system, in which volunteers patrol designated areas in the community and report any drug activity to a central telephone service. Speakers have also been invited to discuss the nature of drugs and the various drug programs in operation locally and nationally. The task force was also influential in getting CMHC to hire a community organizer to work with community groups on the narcotics problem.

The More Effective Group Teaching group has sponsored a course for teachers and parents, "A Community's Concept of Human Relations." The parents are planning and designing the course, and will lead most of the discussion sessions. Participants will take a tour of the community and will get to meet local shopkeepers, librarians, and others. Teachers enrolled will receive course credit from the Board of Education.

The school-community relations task force has determined which schools have the most severe problems in school community relations, and is developing a plan for consulting with these schools. The group's "courtesy campaign" focuses on how parents should be treated in the schools. This task force is also working on plans to enable students to assume certain decision-making powers in their schools.

The success of the forum has legitimized the instrumented laboratory within this community and paved the way for organizational development activity on a community-wide scale. The authors see this as a logical extension of current Organizational Development theory and practice. As a human service organizations become increasingly aware of the need to operate in a community context, new models and plans must be developed to come to grips with this singularly inelegant system. Similarly, those who consult to business organizations might well begin to consider the "community" of consumers as part of their O. D. work.

Significance of Intervention

Certain generalizations from this experience are warranted and may be useful to conference planners.

Entry during conflict: The risks of entering a community conflict situation are great; they seem even greater when the consulting organization invites itself in. Any unsolicited action could easily antagonize a whole client population, thus destroying any effectiveness it might have had in the first place. Whatever the interorganizational dynamics may be in fact, it is clear that a norm within this local community, and one that seems pervasive in our society, is to stay out of a fight unless you're a principal to it or until you're invited in. The paradigm for this attitude is the battling husband and wife who join forces to oppose the policeman summoned by the sounds of their violence. In advance of the forum CMHC staff experienced anxiety on several counts: they feared that no one would attend the forum; that CMHC staff would "blow" the implementation; and even that one or another of the parties to the conflict would picket the forum or otherwise create an organized disruption. That none of these catastrophes occurred is due in part to careful planning and to the design of the forum itself, and in part to the fact that staff apprehensions stemmed more from pervasive norms shared with parties to the conflict than from the realities of group dynamics.

Statutory Relationships: Unlike the private consulting firm which operates in a relatively free market, accepting contracts that satisfy its needs and rejecting those that do not, a community mental health center, supported as it is by tax funds, is obliged to limit its clientele to agencies and organizations within its designated catchment area. The statutory nature of the relationship differentiates the activity of CMHC from the in-house consulting-training unit as well. The actual relationship between a center and its clientele may be thought of as midway between those extremes—more akin to the marriage relationship than the love affair. The parties to it are in a no-exit situation. Some of the implications of this sort of relationship are a reduction in glamour, an increment in mutual dependency and, because of the dependency, a multiplication of the risks of termination. In this context, the relationship established between the CMHC and the local education system during the previous year had some of the characteristics of courtship. The fact that many school system members gave only token support to the forum (a community-directed action) and, at the district level, behaved as if the collaboration between CMHC and Local Group was a flirtation, thus becomes comprehensible. For example, during the two evenings, only three out of a possible 12 district level representatives attended: one refused to participate, and another departed early—the only person present to do so.

There is no way of predicting the long term consequences of the CMHC-school system relationship. The alternatives open in either the in-house or free-market situation (firing, termination of contract, and so on) are clearly not available here. The two parties must continue together. In the immediate post-forum period, the form of the relationship was primarily one of mutual avoidance. One of the three local boards is still at odds with CMHC in spite of efforts to lessen the difficulties. These strains will continue to exist until the school system and its clients are able to shift attention from territorial prerogatives to educational accomplishment. The popular election of local board members to take place during this school year may be a step in this direction.

High turnout: The size of the turnout for the forum was strikingly large. Approximately 150 of the 250 people specifically invited attended. This was due partly to systematic telephone and personal contact, and partly to the urgency of the situation. In a significant sense, however, the result was the product of hundreds of hours of personal contact between CMHC's community organization staff and residents of the community over a period of a year. The level of cooperation between Local Group and CMHC was high: Local Group did the bulk of the telephoning to community members; CMHC aided in bringing out teachers and administrators. Had the forum been sponsored solely by CMHC, it would have been impossible to tap the informal social network of community residents that produced the high turnout.

The design itself: The most unusual features of the forum design were (a) the warm-up period, in which significant group-building interaction began immediately, short-circuiting clique formation and other distancing maneuvers; and (b) the translation of a laboratory intergroup exercise into a format that works in a community conflict situation. It is probable that the translation was successful because the content of the exercise had high face validity (i.e., it permitted discussion of the very educational issues that brought people to the meeting), and because the warm-up period helped the groups develop to the minimum level of solidarity necessary to carry out the exercise.

These two factors suggest at least partial applicability of the forum to other conflict situations. Certainly the lab-like situation can be used in other contexts; some thinking and process are transferable. The authors used the same format to help a suburban New York school group define educational priorities and find ways to study and take action. It was felt that this meeting was less successful, for although face validity was high, the smaller units were not natural—members were strangers and their interests diffuse. The conclusion is that each intervention must be geared to the nature of the group.

Reporting these results: Preparing this report in itself raises some issues of professional ethics and determinants of professional effectiveness. The forum was successful largely because of a trusting relationship between CMHC and many members of Local Group was developed over a substantial period of time. One of the conditions of that relationship is that the scientific and career-building interests of CMHC are subordinate to community service. For this reason the authors refrained from suggesting systematic data collection for research purposes. Although CMHC is working toward evaluation of its programs, with community groups taking a major role in designing and implementing studies, the authors felt that, under these particular circumstances, it was best to avoid risking a loss of trust which might have resulted from any kind of data collection. The hope is that when members of the Local Group (who must necessarily remain anonymous) read this article, they will not feel that this condition has been violated.

SECTION IV

TRAINING

GROUP

DISCUSSION

LEADERS

Your Group Leaders Need Training

EDITH WHITFIELD SEASHORE

There is a new concept in the role of discussion leader. His job is to service the group, and it takes special training for him to understand his function and gain facility in the use of new group techniques. Leader training covers eight areas.

Small discussion groups, now featured quite regularly on programs of large conferences, are inviting a fair amount of criticism. Conference-goers often feel that groups are a waste of time. They feel that more can be accomplished in the lobby, at the bar, in the coffee shop—in small discussion groups of their own making.

Basis For Criticism

Unfortunately, there is some basis for this critcism. Many of us have attended discussion-group sessions in which we have heard such remarks as "It isn't clear why we are meeting," "Nobody knows what we are talking about," "We are pooling ignorance," "Everybody talks about his own problems," "One person dominates the discussion," "We aren't accomplishing anything at all," "The whole thing is a colossal waste of time."

Off the Ground

Of course, some discussion groups do get off the ground, but too many do not. Yet, why shouldn't people be able to come together and think through problems of common concern?

Reprinted by special permission of SALES MEETINGS Magazine and of the author.

What happens to people who ordinarily have a great deal to say to one another when they are assigned to a group and are supposed to meet for a couple of hours? Why do so many groups fail, become paralyzed, or go into a state of chaos?

Perhaps there is too much pressure on the group to produce. Perhaps the members are not interested in the topic. Perhaps the setting is an uncomfortable one.

But what if the discussion group were to consider a problem that concerned the participants, one for which no expert had the answers, but they themselves had the ideas? What if the participants had received background materials before the session and had all heard the same opening talk designed to stimulate their thinking? And what if the participants were assigned to a room where the setting was pleasant and the chairs were comfortable? Would they not then have a more satisfying experience? Undoubtedly they would.

Get Bogged Down

But even with the best physical conditions, a topic of vital interest, and appropriate people present, too many groups get bogged down and stay that way. Why? What is the missing element? The missing element is a person whose responsibility it is to help the group get off the ground and go somewhere. It is the person who can service the group—a discussion leader.

This is a rather new concept—a discussion leader who is a servant to the group. Generally, we tend to think of the leader as the person who has all the answers, the one who is supposed to be 10 steps ahead of other members, the person who can lead the group through a successful session. What an impossible job this is, except perhaps for a few very rare individuals.

However, if the discussion leader thinks of his job as one of rendering service, it need not be an impossible one. But it would become a job for which he would need to be prepared. He would need training in these areas in which he could service the group:

1. Getting the group started
2. Seeing that members become acquainted
3. Selecting topics for discussion
4. Setting discussion priorities and the time to be spent on topics

5. Helping to keep the discussion distributed
6. Handling members who talk too much or do not talk at all or get the group off the topic
7. Summarizing the discussion
8. Planning for following sessions.

How can a leader be prepared to give his group help in these areas? There are a number of ways, but one method is a leaders' training session, held the day before the conference.

This kind of session can take many forms. One of the most acclaimed patterns is a day-long session with experts skilled in training discussion leaders. (Experts such as these often are available through universities and the NTL Institute.) All the leaders should be heartily encouraged to attend. Many organizations pay their expenses for the day. To do the job well, conference planners have found that a leader's training session takes time and costs money but that it pays off in a number of important ways.

Not only are leaders better prepared to serve their groups, but the organization will have gained a commitment from them toward helping to make the conference a more productive experience, and particularly a commitment to the small discussion groups, which may comprise a large part of the program.

From the leaders' point of view, the gains also are manifold, including, of course, acquiring skills which have a much wider use than merely to serve their conference groups.

It is amazing to find how receptive executives can be to a training session if they see it as a briefing session and essential to fulfilling their job with the discussion groups, and not solely as a session to train them in how to lead discussions. Usually they consider themselves quite expert in this role. Even if they think otherwise, in all likelihood they will not talk about it and most certainly will not admit to needing help. But they *will* come to be briefed, and if the session is well planned, they will go away briefed—and trained.

Leaders will come to sessions with numerous specific questions concerning the conference to which they want answers. Therefore, their briefing should include a thorough orientation session with the conference planners as well as other sessions devoted to conference details.

They will also come to the briefing sessions with a number

of concerns which they should have a chance to talk over
with one another:

"How much of the content will the group expect me to know?"

"How much do I have to know in order to feel secure?"

"What are some of the things I can do if the group gets jammed
up?"

"What if nobody talks?"

"Suppose people want to change to another group?"

"How do we choose a recorder for the group?"

Suggested Leaders' Training Session

During briefing sessions, leaders should meet in small
practice groups to talk over their concerns and to practice
ways of helping the group—of working with members.

A leaders' training-session program might look like this:

*(It is the day before a conference at which about 600 participants
are expected to register. Sixty leaders have been selected and are
meeting for the day with three or four trainers.)*

9 A.M.—OPENING SESSION

A conference official welcomes leaders. Conference planners
describe in detail the conference program and the rationale
behind it. The job of the discussion leaders is described. After
the leaders have a look at the conference and their job, they
spend some time discussing the program and the sessions
with which they will be involved.

10:30 A.M.-12:30 P.M.

The remainder of the morning is a combination of some work
with the large group of leaders and some work in small
practice sessions of 15-20 leaders, with each small group
having a trainer.

In the large-group session, leaders look briefly at the topic
the discussion groups will take up first when they convene.
They then watch a hypothetical group as it starts its meeting,
so that they can see some of the areas in which they will be
called on to serve their groups.

In the small practice sessions, leaders form their own
agenda of the topics with which they are concerned and then
spend the session in discussing these topics and trying out
different ways of working with the problems they will encounter in serving their groups.

1 P.M.—LUNCHEON

2:30-5 P.M.

The total group also has an afternoon session in which leaders can talk through more of the content which the groups will be considering.

A practice session of at least two hours follows, during which the small groups, with a trainer, continue to pursue their own agenda.

6 P.M.—DINNER

7:30-9:30 P.M.

An evening session is desirable, particularly in order to continue work in the small practice groups.

The last half hour of the evening is spent with the total group of leaders meeting together to get a thorough briefing on the various details with which they will be involved:

1. The materials the group members will receive
2. The person to contact if the room becomes overheated
3. The location of the rest rooms
4. The hours for the leaders' meetings, at which they will report on the activity of their groups
5. Their own group and room assignments.

This is a picture of a day-long training session. But if the conference is a short one and there is less briefing of leaders to be done, the training session could also be shorter— possibly only half a day. Conversely, some training sessions have been longer, even two or three days in length. But generally, whatever the length, the pattern is similar to the one-day program outlined above.

With this kind of preparation, discussion leaders should be prepared to fill the missing element of helping conference participants to feel that the time spent in discussion groups, featured on the conference program, was time well spent, not wasted.

And the organization will benefit from this well-spent time by having a membership which has become more involved and has found sessions both productive and enjoyable.

A Design for Training Discussion Leaders

BETTY R. ELLIS and

W. WARNER BURKE

Recently the NTL Institute received a request for consultation regarding a conference on faculty desegregation in the public schools of Dade County (Miami), Florida. The Dade County Classroom Teachers Association was planning a one and one-half-day conference for 500 participants and wanted small-group discussion as an integral part of the design. Along with Sam Ethridge of NEA, they were wondering whether NTL could "transform" some 26 teachers, supervisors, librarians, and assistant principals into group discussion leaders prior to the conference. They also requested that the NTL consultants help plan the conference, and see it through along with the group leaders.

This kind of request certainly is not a new one. During the late '40's and early '50's Leland Bradford, Kenneth Benne, Ronald and Gordon Lippitt, and others were called upon to help plan more effective conferences. The main emphasis was on active participation instead of passive attention to an army of speakers. In the middle '50's Richard Beckhard and Edith (Whitfield) Seashore became NTL's experts on conference planning, implementation, and evaluation. They also became NTL's source for training group discussion leaders.

If the events of recent months are any indication NTL is once again in the business of training group discussion leaders and helping to plan conferences. In addition to the Florida conference, an identical one has been conducted in Nashville, Tennessee. Two consultants trained group discussion leaders for two and one-half days prior to a one and

169

Reprinted by special permission from HUMAN RELATIONS TRAINING NEWS, Volume 11, Number 2.

one-half-day conference, or seminar, in which the newly trained leaders employed their learnings. The trainers remained during the conference to provide consultation for the discussion leaders. This article focuses on the two and one-half days of leadership training.

The emphasis for the first day of training was on group problem solving and specific group processes. By the end of the day, the leaders were becoming increasingly aware of the skills necessary in the problem-solving process and increasingly conscious of their own strengths and weaknesses in the group discussion situation. The third day was divided into two major parts. The first part involved further training in group process plus a "wrap-up" lecture on effective group discussion leadership. The second half of the day was needed for administrative matters before the conference began at 4:00 p.m.

These two training events followed fairly closely the emphases of previous training designs for group discussion leadership. When Richard Beckhard and Edith Whitfield were training leaders, the notion of full group-member participation was fairly innovative and the main focus was on group process. The training sessions reported here also stressed group processes—interpersonal communication, high participation vs. silent members, and so on. In addition, because the conference dealt with faculty desegregation, the trainers felt that group problem-solving skills also needed to be accentuated.

The Training Design

The opening exercise consisted of asking the participants to write what their expectations were. These expectations were discussed in trios, then one participant from each trio shared the thoughts with the entire group. One of the trainers recorded the name, sex, and race of each individual in order to divide the participants into heterogeneous groups. Following a coffee break, the group was divided into the four subgroups which were to be workgroups for the remainder of the training conference. During each workgroup session, each group selected a leader and a recorder. Each group had at its disposal a dittoed record of the previous session, newsprint emphasizing the major points, and a tape recorder. Their first task, following a brief theory session on problem solving, was to state the problems of faculty desegregation.

After they had met for one hour, they discussed the work-group products in a general session. The discussion focused on the distinction between problems and solutions and pointed up the phenomenon that groups usually jump to solutions without appropriately identifying the problem.

In a general session after lunch, the one-way/two-way communication exercise was conducted. The main point emphasized was that effective interpersonal communication is a function of establishing a common frame of reference. To provide practice in this area, in the next workgroup meeting each group member paraphrased what the previous speaker had said before making his own point. This exercise proved to be fairly frustrating, but the point that effective listening is an active process rather than a passive one was well made. The workgroups spent the remainder of the afternoon in further problem identification. The last input was a personal inquiry[1] concerning participants' experiences that day.

The second day began with a theory session on force-field analysis. Each workgroup then constructed a force-field analysis on problems of faculty desegregation in their area. After a number of forces were listed, each group took a separate force element and began planning action steps to increase the driving force or decrease the restraining force. Before this period, the trainers asked one member in each group to play a "silent member" role, i.e., not to participate in the discussion unless specifically asked to do so. A reaction scale was administered following the session. The silent members' reactions to the session were compared with the other members' reactions on such dimensions as satisfaction, responsibility, commitment, and frustration. The feedback data showed that the silent members felt less satisfaction, responsibility, and commitment than the other members and that they experienced greater frustration. A short lecture on the importance of group-member participation and involvement concluded the session.

The final session for the day was a role-playing exercise in which the imaginary setting was the first meeting of their small group at the conference that would begin the next afternoon. Eight of the 24 members took part in a demonstration with the rest of the group as observers. The eight

---

[1] A copy of this questionnaire may be obtained from W. Warner Burke, NTL Institute.

participants were assigned to play various stereotypes which could be present in their groups. Assigned roles varied widely from real-life roles: whites played Negroes and Negroes played whites, in education, training, and current professional assignments. One member was trained to help the participants warm up in their parts. Because of the high emotion generated, a great deal of time was spent discussing the emotional reactions of the observers as well as the role interactions.

The final half-day opened with a group-observer group session. Since the groups were still the regular workgroups, a discussion leader and a recorder were selected. The task of the "inside" group was to discuss what they had learned about effective leadership in group discussion, especially what to do and what not to do. The task of the "outside" group was to observe the group's progress and later give them feedback. This exercise served several purposes. It clarified perceptions regarding effective qualities they saw their fellow trainees as possessing; it provided an arena for sharing the "action" decisions of each trainee for the opening of his own discussion group; and it provided further opportunity for understanding group process. The remainder of the time was spent on actual preplanning for the conference. This consisted mainly of administrative detail, including group assignments and legitimizing an interim session and a postconference session for the leaders. An evaluation questionnaire was filled out by the discussion leaders at this time.

The conference itself consisted of speakers and small-group discussions. There were three small-group meetings, ranging in time from 90 minutes to three hours. Although a general "charge" was given before each small-group meeting, there was considerable flexibility as to the specific topics for discussion or problem solving. The minutes of each small group were dittoed and made available to the other discussion leaders to provide ideas for their own groups.

Evaluation

The evaluation of this training design can best be discussed at three levels: (1) the written evaluation by the discussion leaders; (2) the observations of the trainers in relation to the techniques actually used by the discussion leaders and the problems discussed in the postsession; (3) the evaluation day one month following the Nashville conference.

There were seven questions on the evaluation form completed by the discussion leaders. The first four questions asked for a response on a 7-point scale concerning the value of the training. The remaining three were open-ended questions on how the training could be improved. The first question requested information on the personal value of the training. Twenty of the 24 trainees rated the training as "highly valuable," the highest rating. The second question, dealing with the length of the training, showed a split between "about right" and "moderately short." The third question dealt with the relevance of this training to other situations. Twenty-two of the 24 rated it "very useful." The fourth question, dealing with the perception of how well they would have performed without the training, produced responses dispersed over six of the seven points on the scale. The feeling in general seemed to fluctuate around 4, "as well as the next person"; and 3, "moderately poor."

(The Miami trainees reacted favorably to basically the same questions, but their ratings were, on the average, one point lower on each scale. Perhaps the slight changes in the design for the two and one-half-day Nashville program were beneficial.)

The fifth question, requesting information on the "least useful" part of the design, produced limited response. Three trainees felt that better use could have been made of the tape recorders in small-group sessions. The sixth question asked what aspects of the training could be better emphasized or clarified. The feedback on this item indicated that more clarification was needed on basic goals. It was also suggested that more role playing and clustering would be valuable. The last question dealt with suggestions for the future. Seven trainees suggested either one or two additional days' training time. Other responses centered around more time on specific skills.

As consultants during the desegregation conference and the postsession meetings, we were able to see what training experiences had been effective. One example was that the stereotypes depicted in the role play during the training became realities to the discussion leaders within their own conference groups. Another example was that two discussion leaders invented an evaluation instrument which they administered to their groups. Three discussion leaders used the tape recorders during the sessions and then listened to them to gain insights to use in their next session. Force-field analysis and problem-solving techniques were used in every group. Each of the 24 groups did a force-field analysis of the desegregation problem as it related to his area of the country. At the suggestion of the consultants, each leader reproduced the analysis for his own use as well as for the other groups.

In the middle of the conference the discussion leaders in Nashville hired a photographer to photograph various stages of the training and the conference for use in a proposed publication entitled "The Nashville Story." The success of the conference led the cosponsoring agencies—the NEA Committee on Professional Rights and Responsibilities and the Metropolitan Nashville Education Association—to plan an evaluation session for one month later.

At the evaluation session it was immediately evident that the discussion leaders had formed a tightly knit group that wished to work on many educational problems.

By the end of the day plans were being made in four areas. First, teams were established to explore possibilities for further funding to their professional organization by the Federal government. Second, all the leaders were actively exploring ways to become more active in their professional organization. Third, they discussed the first draft of "The Nashville Story."[2] Fourth, subteams were established to explore the possibilities of working on many problems the association had identified for study this year. They were particularly interested in working in the area of inservice education.

Living through the Miami and Nashville experiences, we could see the limitations and the assets in the training design. In both experiences, the participants felt that an initial overview of the two and one-half-day training period would have been helpful. More training time might have been useful. The assets of the program speak for themselves, especially through the discussion leaders' evaluations. Furthermore, both groups have planned follow-up programs, with continuing use of NTL consultants.

---

2 In report of the National Education Association Professional Rights and Responsibilities Committee on Civil and Human Rights of Educators, Faculty Desegregation Conferences. Available on request.